Tapestry Of Roots:

Threads Woven By The Master

Tapestry Of Roots:

Threads Woven By The Master

Angela Phelan

Messianic Publishers, LLC

Cover Design by Amy Wilkes

Published by Messianic Publishers, LLC
Memphis, Tennessee U.S.A.

Books are available at:
www.tapestryofrootsorders.com

ISBN - 978-0-9888920-9-5

Unless otherwise noted, all Scripture quotations in this publication are from the Holy Bible, ESV Version © 2005. Scriptures used by permission.

Dedication

To the Church, that she cherish the roots of her faith
and embrace her Savior cloaked in His full identity.

Acknowledgments

This book represents years of searching and a passion to weave the true heart of our Jewish Messiah into the folds of His church. What began for me as a simple quest for the roots of the Christian faith transformed into a deeper, more intimate relationship with our Father. For the hours of teaching and discipleship at B'rit Hadasha Messianic Jewish Synagogue, I will be forever grateful. My life has been changed in ways too numerous to recount, and His heart has flowed forth through each person present. As the Lord placed this book upon my heart, He has been faithful to provide all things necessary each step of the process. From the one who reached out and offered help when his plate was already full to the publisher who immediately embraced the mission placed before us, He has remained forever near. Words cannot express my gratitude to Chad Holland for his continual support, encouragement, and review of this writing, and most importantly, for the teachings which have formed much of the basis of this book. My most sincere thanks go also to Frances McCampbell, always present as a ray of encouragement and hope, for catching the vision of this book and bringing it to print. As time came to actually enclose the manuscript within a cover, He brought Amy Wilkes, who transformed a general idea into a beautiful cover. Thank you, my friend. Gratitude abounds also for countless friends, who have patiently endured sessions of teaching and who have supported and prayed through the years this book has journeyed. For my dear family, I love you more than words could ever express. You have each shared in my vision and allowed me to steal away to the park each week to be with my Father and capture His heart. I stand truly humbled, honored, and thankful to be a part of His plan.

Contents

Forward

"Angela Phelan's book on the Covenants of God exposes the deepest motives of God's heart for His creation. Step by step and generation after generation, God has consistently been pursuing faithful men and women to offer covenant relationships to; in some instances with individuals, and at other times with nations. In this book, Angela is able to identify how God seeks a deep and intimate relationship with us by giving us relevant background information and Biblical examples of how God pursued and related with Israel and the Jewish people historically. Knowing that God's calling for His people is irrevocable (Romans 11:29), the important fact that Israel is again a nation and that Jewish people have been preserved through many trials, proves God's covenant making and covenant keeping nature.

In many ways, God's plan of redemption and His desired end result of a redeemed creation is shown one piece at a time in how He offers covenant relationships to the patriarchs of faith and to us today. I believe this book will open the eyes and hearts of those who have not already seen God in His true light. God created us out of desire to relate intimately and shows Himself to be consistently open to go deeper with those that want to go deeper with Him (James 4:8)."

Pastor Chad Holland
King Of Kings Community
Jerusalem, Israel

"….. remember

it is not you who support the root

but the root that supports you."

Romans 11:18 ESV

Introduction

So, a book about covenant?

In these days of instant messaging, chat, and texts, why should anyone care about covenants? With conversations and photos traversing miles in milli-seconds, who could want more? Aren't we more connected than ever before? Aren't our relationships stronger with each press of the key?

Why even give a fleeting thought to such an aged concept? After all, what possible relevance could it hold to a world moving at light speed, interconnected, and accessing a world of knowledge beneath their fingertips?

Really, isn't covenant an antiquated term, dusty with Biblical lore and withering away into obscurity?

*   *   *   *   *   *   *   *   *

But wait, perhaps a lingering fragment of relativity remains tucked snuggly beneath a dusty cover, an underlying need for all this interaction and connectivity.   Perhaps?   Could it be a need for relationships, a pull within each of us to connect with others, to feel valued and loved, to belong and have worth?

Still don't see a relation to covenant?   Be patient. Put aside the fleeting world swirling around and consider a few scenarios.

Contemplate with me the pull of relationship, that which is fulfilling and beneficial as well as that which may be destructive or detrimental.   What is that innermost feeling, that desire to connect, to thrive, to be loved, that draws us together?   What often blinds the eyes and draws the heart, propelling the oppressed back again and again despite all reason?   Why do some cling and grasp with fists clenched to relationships wrought with destruction, holding until blood streams from hands raw?

Relationship. Hope. Fear. Fear of losing *the relationship*, fear greater than the pain slaying within. That tug, that draw of relationship is almost impossible to resist.

Until…..

Until the truth begins to shine through a crevice, a crack worn and misshapen. A still, quiet voice whispers *rebirth, redemption, restoration, relationship.* As His breath flows, truth illumines, transforming fractures into works of art designed for His glory and purpose. Because of His perfect design, the pull of relationship wields such force.

Now, travel with me to a different scenario, one found currently within any number of churches.

Lingering quietly among the pews is a feeling that something is missing, that perhaps the church is not functioning as it should or in a way which would reap the most growth and development for its members while drawing those on the outside. Hovering below the rafters and stain glass windows floats a current of unrest, searching, and a desire to walk out faith differently. A generalized feeling of lack, thirst, and hunger for more is almost palpable as we go about the apparent functions of our faith. Rather than walking aimlessly forward, we desire to tread with intention and to know God's love and will for us within our very core, without any hesitation whatsoever. Seeking to discover that which would bring a closer *relationship* with our Father and provide renewed nourishment for our souls, we wait. We search. We yearn for more. We question. Is this all? We hope for a glimpse of His glory and presence as we traverse our daily paths, seeking always for evidence of that which we do not see and which seems often to rest just beyond reach. We long to feel His presence, to hear His quiet voice, and to rest assured in His mighty arms …. to experience Him.

But, how can we truly experience Him when we have forgotten the essence of His being, when we have traveled a path of our own design? We have lost the beat of His heart, the life of His breath, the way designed for *relationship* with Him. We have missed a fundamental part of our faith, our *relationship* with the very Creator of the universe. We have forgotten His covenant.

Covenant. There it is again. Why must this be so pervasive, the pull of *relationship* so strong? Why are we constantly seeking, longing for that which seems so infrequently obtained and rests often beyond grasp? What is that drive, that need for something more, that feeling that something is lacking or missing? For what are we searching? *Relationship*. The heart of our Father.

Although most often understood as an agreement between parties, the true essence of a covenant is the *relationship* underlying the agreement. We have lost sight of His true heart, His desire for us. We have sought, questioned, and waited, and we have missed the still, quiet voice drawing our hearts. In His infinite knowledge, the Almighty prepared a template for us by which we may prosper within the context of relationships with others and with Himself. A perfect design lies wrapped within the dusty pages and age old concept of covenant, a perfect plan to provide that which is missing, to quench the searching which fills our days, to provide a place of peace, acceptance, and love unlike any other. This pull, drawing, searching has been placed by Him within our very core, so that we might seek Him and thrive in *relationship*. Because of His perfect design, relationships wield such force.

Covenant. Are you beginning to see?

Years ago, I sat amongst those church pews, longing to truly experience Him yet feeling that something was missing, an integral piece of His design. Words flowed through my spirit, suggesting that I didn't know His heart within my core, that there was so much more He longed to reveal. I lingered for years despite the draw, feeling that tug within my spirit, the voice of a patient and loving Father in pursuit of His child. I searched, prayed, and served, yet the pull remained; that still, quiet voice whispered. How He patiently waited, yearning to reveal the entirety of His person, to disclose untold intricacies, and to exhale the breath of life exhibited through relationship true and pure. As His voice stirred within, I was drawn to seek a greater knowledge of Him, to investigate the heritage of our Savior and the roots of Christianity. As awareness dawned, the missing piece shone forth.

Where was the Jewish Messiah in all His glorious and rich heritage?

Why was our Savior a Jew?

A nagging sense of incompleteness began to grow within my spirit. I longed to truly discover the basis of my faith, to investigate the beginnings of Christianity, and to understand the chasm which exists between Christianity and the Jewish community. Feeling a restlessness and a desire to fully absorb all aspects of my Savior, I was drawn to a Messianic Jewish congregation seven years ago. Contrary to Orthodox Jewish synagogues, Messianic communities are comprised of Jewish and gentile believers who embrace Jesus as their Messiah and Savior but continue to follow the traditional feasts, festivals, and practices which God ordained for His nation. It was at that point that I began to experience *relationship* with Christ as never before, that I found richness and completeness unimaginable, and that I finally began to understand the significance of our Messiah's heritage. Reviewing history through a lens overlaid with Jewish tradition opened my eyes to a Heavenly Father whose love and design for us remains unfathomable, a Father yearning for *relationship*.

Amidst the organs and crosses, the pulpits and pews, have we truly grasped a Jewish Savior and felt the beat of His heart within our own?

Even the smallest detail within His plan carries enormous precision and underlying meaning. Returning to the roots of our faith allows a full script to emerge, beautifully and perfectly written, which solidifies our faith and guides us into closer *relationship* with our Creator. The heart of the Father has beat always for His creation, desiring *relationship* above all. As wayward man has blazed a path of his own choosing, He has stood forever near, pursuing, yearning, and weaving a tapestry of redemption through the ages. The true beat of His heart is covenant.

Do you see it yet?

Covenant … perhaps a lingering relevance remains.

Perhaps there is a reason our world exists dark, misdirected, and self-serving. As life whirls in instant reality, we have lost our way. Despite our obsession with being connected, our relationships are more broken than ever before, wrought with evil, abuse, and motives misguided. Violence and wickedness swirl as the line between right and wrong blurs and even transposes. The instantaneous sharing has failed to truly yield our hearts' desires or quench the thirst which lies within our core. In the face of technological advances unfathomed, the gaping hole within our hearts remains; the innate desire and pull for true relationship remains unsatisfied. A quiet voice whispers in the midst of each split-second pause, begging to be noticed. Fulfillment, acceptance, and validation can't truly be found with the press of a key.

While we strive to be connected, are we really? Are our bonds with others stronger? With each click, we are no closer to that for which we long. How, in a world of advancement inconceivable, have we strayed so? Could there be a better way, a different path? Put aside the world flashing by at light speed and return with me to ages past.

Pause for a brief second and feel His pulse, a heart longing for creation. Inhale the breath He longs to impart. Follow with me the history of covenant, embrace the pull of relationship, and relish the pursuit of a loving Father.

Pull back the cover worn and faded, blow the dust from pages fragile, and delve into the history of His design. Return to the Old Testament, to the beginning of time, to the One who created all with a single desire ..... *relationship*. Feel the beat of His heart, the air of His breath, the longing always for *relationship*. Trace the thread of covenant and grasp with entirety the depth wrapped within the simple word. To understand fully the heart of the Father, you must journey through ages past and revisit the concept of covenant and relationship through the lens of Jewish heritage.

Glimpse inside an ancient world.

Reconsider covenant ......

Relationship.

Tapestry Of Roots: Threads Woven By The Master

1

The King Of The Jews

Within crude letters carved upon a simple sign, the cornerstone of Christianity was revealed. "Above His head they placed the written charge against Him: This is Jesus, the King of the Jews." Matthew 27:37 NIV. If we would halt our gaze to linger longer upon that rudimentary sign, allowing the entirety of the words to permeate the innermost of our beings, our hearts and eyes could be opened to the richness and beauty woven beneath our faith. Understanding the tapestry of roots which support the Christian faith nourishes and strengthens our souls in a myriad of ways. Just as the roots of a tree form a complex support network for the outward beauty, the tendrils interlaced beneath the surface of Christianity create the foundation upon which our beliefs exist, delivering the nutrients necessary to thrive and complete that which our Heavenly Father has beckoned. Although invisible and lacking in apparent beauty, the roots entwined beneath allow the very existence of the glory and miracles above. The fullness of the Christian faith is revealed when we return to the true origins of that which supports, nourishes, and protects our daily walk with our Father.

So, why was Jesus born a Jew, and what exactly does that signify? Apart from the fulfillment of prophecy, what is the greater meaning, essence, and purpose for the heritage of our Messiah? Unlocking this mystery reveals a world created by divine order in which the enormity of even the smallest detail is inconceivable and carries with it an inner beauty and richness which is indescribable, capable of nourishing our souls as He has longed. Come and drink in fullness the water He has graciously provided, absorb every ounce of sustenance from the tapestry of roots He has woven perfectly beneath our lives, and inhale the richness of the faith which we profess in Jesus, the King of the Jews.

Embodied within the man known as Jesus is the very presence of God Himself, a perfect representation of all that God would envision for those who walk upon our earth. As we look to Jesus as the example for our daily lives, we would be remiss if we failed to consider all aspects of our divine Savior. By looking at our faith through a lens overlaid with the richness and depth which characterize the Jewish heritage of Christ, we awaken to see more fully His heart and divine purpose and plan for all humanity. Within the precepts at the core of our Father's initial relationship with His prize creation, a breathtaking design is unveiled which orchestrates the flow of relationships as He intended, not only with Himself but with a world in desperate need of a savior.

"In the same way, after the supper He took the cup, saying, 'This cup is the new covenant in my blood, which is poured out for you.'" Luke 22:20 NIV. While these words are familiar to most who profess salvation through Jesus, the complexity enveloped within is indescribable if we would only pause and truly breathe in the concept of a covenant. As we allow this simple word to nourish our innermost beings, we discover a principle which permeated every aspect of the lives of the Israelites, for they were a covenant people created to be a nation of priests to the world, chosen uniquely to show God's love and divine order to all things. Following the original sin in the Garden of Eden, God immediately set into motion a plan of redemption, of restoring to man the ability to have close, covenant relationship with Him. Although unfathomable, the Creator of all extended His hand, beckoning His rebellious creation and providing a way to return to fellowship with Him through the institution of covenants. As God extended covenant to all upon the earth through the redemptive blood of Jesus, He longs for us to absorb all that is signified by the offer He so graciously extends. Fully embracing this precept allows us to thrive within the intimate relationships envisioned by our Father and for which we were divinely created.

So, what exactly is a covenant? The roots and essence of Christianity are embedded within this ancient Biblical concept, an age-old principle which remains relevant to this day. Although often thought of as an agreement, the true essence of a covenant is actually the relationship behind the arrangement. It is substantiated with words, a sign, and consequences for adherence and disobedience to the covenant. The lives of the Hebrew people revolved around these concepts, as they lived, breathed, and maintained relationships between themselves and their Heavenly Father.

Just as the faith of the ancient Israelites was centered upon the understanding of covenants, the roots of Christianity intertwine beneath the surface to find nourishment and meaning within this term. As Christians we understand that we are under a new covenant, offered to us through the blood of Jesus. By traveling back through the history of God's chosen people, we see more clearly what is signified by the covenant of salvation offered to us through the sacrificial death of Jesus. Christianity, faith, and salvation are all about covenant. Covenant. Covenant. How many times have we heard this word yet been remiss to give it the consideration it so justly deserves? Allowing this principle to flood our beings and soak into our hearts carries with it strength, refreshment, and the ability to envision God's love and desire for us in a way we have never before imagined. Once we as Christians truly comprehend just what is enveloped within our covenant relationship with our Father, we will be compelled to lead far different lives, lives walked out daily in true relationship with the Almighty full of new-found respect, reverence, and overwhelming love for Him and for those around us. Oh, that we would truly grasp the meaning, experience the all surpassing love of our Father, and that we would in turn be compelled to stretch out our arms in covenant to those within our lives, as modeled to us through our Creator and His Son.

2

Covenant

Created in the very image of God, we are designed to live and prosper within the context of covenants and relationships. As remarkable creations of the Most High, we are molded to be a portrayal of the very essence of God, crafted with purpose and intentionality to live within intimate fellowship with our Creator. Our Father is One abounding with love, unchanging in devotion, and desirous of relationships with those to whom He offered the breath of life. He is also the God of ultimate control, One who effortlessly orchestrates the very confines of time and weaves all of creation together to accomplish His purpose. With our Heavenly Father, nothing is left to chance or random occurrence. From the beginning of time, He has provided us with all things necessary to prosper and live within the fellowship He so desires. The understanding of a covenant world necessitates an accepting of relationships as the building blocks upon which society is constructed.

Our Heavenly Father in His infinite love searches for ways to make covenant with His creation, to demolish the walls of transgressions we have allowed to separate us from the path to which He has called. The very nature of our beings and our desire to usurp His ultimate control have made the institution of covenants a necessity. As we struggle against our innate desire for self-rule, covenants provide the standards, clarification, and expectations with regard to how we should conduct our lives.

While a covenant is often considered to be merely an

agreement between two parties, its true essence lies within the relationship signified by the expression. Through words, the foundation of the relationship is confirmed, establishing terms which set forth mutual blessings for adherence as well as repercussions for any violations. This attention to detail allows the relationship to stay on track and to function as the parties intended, allowing both parties to thrive. Finally, the covenant is marked with a sign, calling to remembrance the significance of the relationship and providing the accountability necessary to insure the relationship continues along the path which was initially envisioned. Covenant principles carry with them the expectation that each party involved will withhold nothing from the other, even to the point of life if necessary. To truly follow covenant ideals, one must be willing to lay down his life for the other, adhering to the covenant at all cost. The whole of our existence is substantiated, brought to fruition, and woven intricately together through friendship, love, obedience, and relationship. Each strand relies and builds upon each other, creating a masterpiece woven in the image of our Father.

To understand fully what is expected of a covenant relationship we need only to look at our Heavenly Father and the relationships He so thoroughly desires for His creation. Although entirely undeserving, we as believers have been rescued from a life of certain peril through the outstretched hand of abounding love extended by the Creator of the entire universe. As He rescues us from impending demise, the hand offered is one of unchanging surety, founded upon a love unimaginable. His love is boundless, His grasp secure, and His ways and character remain steadfast throughout the passage of time. Although unfathomable, the Creator withholds absolutely nothing from His unworthy creation, even to the point of His Son. From sin's first entrance, He set into motion our redemption, knowing fully what it would require, yet desiring the restoration of relationship with us above all. He is the creator not only of all things but also of perfect, enduring relationships. In providing His Son, God models for us absolute, pure love born out of complete vulnerability. Through His laws and statutes, He lovingly provides a pathway for us to travel so that we might bask in His protection and absorb the fulfillment of relationships as He has envisioned. Although seemingly contrary to our human nature, laws were instituted for us, to fully illustrate the impossibility of living a righteous life on our own and to exemplify the need for a savior. The ancient Israelites saw the Law as good, as provided by a loving God who desired only the best for His people. God is a God of covenant, and His people understood everything signified within that simple word. As a covenant keeping Creator, our Father reveals to us the meaning for our very existence, to grow and to expand His kingdom through our relationships with our Savior and those along our paths.

Once we truly comprehend the nature of our Father and allow the depth of His love and divine plan to infiltrate our minds and souls, a breathtaking picture emerges which illuminates the perfect design for relating to God and our world through covenant. Just as He rescued us from a life of sin and rebellion, we are to approach others with the same love. We are to be unchanging, keepers of our word, striving always to maintain meaning and permanence within our word and actions. As we endeavor to submit fully to our Lord daily, we must also be willing to yield our wishes and desires to those around, to lay down our lives if necessary to those with whom we hold covenant.

Let us be a people truly created to live according to covenant principles, a people steadfast in honor, commitment, and love. Let us be the unique who remain firm in the midst of the storms of life, who remain unchanging in a world of constant transformations and turmoil. Although people vary and circumstances fluctuate, let our love for others remain steady as we strive always to be the one upon which they can rely. Let us demonstrate our Savior to the world, be strikingly different from the waves that constantly crash against us, and point always to the Cornerstone upon whom all may safely build their lives. As we model our Savior to a world in such need, may we reflect a willingness to be vulnerable, to place others' interests ahead of our own, and to lay down our lives for them as Christ did for us. A world currently unrecognizable would spring forth if we would place ourselves under covenantal principles bringing infinite respect, value, love, and honor to even the seemingly least of these. Only then will we truly see the purpose of relationship as He intended, absorb the beauty of community He envisioned, and capture and inhale just a fraction of the boundless love He has for us. The kingdom of God and the meaning of our existence is rooted within the model of covenant.

3

A Covenant World

"This is my commandment, that you love one another as I have loved you. Greater love has no one than this, that someone lay down his life for his friends. You are my friends if you do what I command you. No longer do I call you servants, for the servant does not know what his master is doing; but I have called you friends, for all that I have heard from my Father I have made known to you." John 15:12-15 ESV.

Through the words of Jesus, the importance of relationships and obedience are emphasized once again. Embodied within the flesh of man, our Heavenly Father allows a glimpse into His very nature while providing the perfect example for us to follow. Love others as Christ has loved us, withholding nothing from each other, even to the point of our lives. True, covenant principled friendship is centered not upon ourselves, but rather upon our Father and those He has brought within our circles. Jesus continues by stating that we are friends; no longer are we servants, for we know what the Father is doing. He has provided us with a meticulous design for relating to Himself and to those who walk along our paths. How our Father longs for us to absorb the concepts wrapped within a covenant and to follow the paths He has outlined before us.

A true friend is a beautiful illustration of the ideals which comprise the meaning of a covenant. Love within a covenant world is genuine and pure, borne of a desire to see the other thrive and grow within the calling placed upon him by the Father.

In doing so, we place the interests of the other person ahead of our own, desiring the finest for them and choosing to believe the best of them always. True love is a choice, for genuine love does not abound where choice is forbidden. Our loving Father always supplies us with a choice and leaves us with the assurance that even if we wander astray, He will provide a way back through repentance and obedience. As the Creator of all, God allowed Adam and Eve access to two trees in the Garden of Eden and extended an offer of trust wrapped within the trees' existence. Desirous of obedience and love above all and in spite of the personal cost, He provided man with a choice.

When considering a world based upon covenants, we are confronted with a myriad of ideas exceedingly contrary to our very beings. Loving another to the point of laying down your life if necessary, placing another's interests ahead of your own, and offering your absolute all to another are covenant principles which immediately cause us to pause and consider the true cost involved. Our Heavenly Father, overflowing with love unimaginable, has withheld nothing from His unworthy creation, and He longs for us to live according to the example He has graciously provided. Within a covenant, you find loyalty, devotion, and humility in the absence of self-interest; such qualities extend beyond the original parties to encompass the families and descendants of those to whom covenant is extended. To live within a covenant, it must have first been offered to you. If we could truly grasp the enormity of the love enveloped within the covenant offered to us through Jesus, we would be moved to reach out to others with the same acceptance and love.

Also woven within the concept of a covenant is the expectation of obedience to our Heavenly Father and to the terms established within the agreement. Covenantal living carries with it a degree of accountability, as the conditions clearly delineate the appropriate actions if the agreement is broken. Within the covenants most familiar to us, the terms of the relationship are established on the front end, as expectations are noted and violations are considered. Living within a covenant community requires us as Christians to maintain the highest standard of accountability and to be keepers of our word rather than mere speakers. If we would truly shine as the light we were destined to be and remain steadfast in our Father throughout the storms of life, we would live in a world vastly different from our current reality. Holding firm to our Savior and the promises contained within Scripture would usher in hope, meaning, and light to a world replete with darkness and despair longing for a sense of relevancy. How our Heavenly Father must yearn for us to live each day in remembrance of the One who has given His all to return to the fellowship envisioned with creation's breath. If we as Christians would truly live in accordance with the New Covenant of our salvation, binding His words and commands as frontlets between our eyes, we would be moved to reach out to a world in desperate need of a savior.

Covenant relationships carry with them a degree of permanence, of continuance of honor and respect which extend to further generations. The ancient Israelites operated within the confines of covenant, identifying themselves through a series of relationships defined by their tribe, clan, family, and father. By recounting these primary relationships, they were able to discern any covenantal agreements which had been previously established and which would provide security, respect, or honor among apparent strangers. One would treat the descendants of a covenant relationship with the same principles initially established with the original person. Covenants carried with them the expectations of mutual respect, honor, love, and permanence which extended across generations.

The Hebrew people lived and thrived within small communities centered upon covenants, and they carried these familiar concepts with them as the development of local synagogues began to emerge. A return to such a lifestyle would allow renewed vision and intentionality to spring forth while calling to remembrance our Father's faithfulness, devotion, and love. If we lived within the context of small interworking communities worshipping together in local congregations, we would possess a sense of community and commonality rarely found today. Our calling of making disciples, following, and serving our Savior would shine forth and draw others into the fold. If we viewed ourselves as the church instead of identifying the church as a place where we go, our entire vision of how our lives operate would be altered. Dr. Michael Schiffmann in *Return of the Remnant* identifies the word *church* as being a translation through Latin of the Greek word *ekklesia* which means to call out. Originally, *ekklesia* stems from the Hebrew word *Qahal*, which means to call.[1] Further elaboration on the Hebrew translation notes the background of church as being *Kehillah/congregation*. Rather than being a building where weekly service is held, the true essence of a church is a congregation, a people, called out to serve, follow, and illustrate our Father to the world around. We should be a network of believers intertwined with covenant principles which guide our every action and shine forth from the core of our beings. Recognizing our Heavenly Father as the One from whom all things flow, we within the congregations should work within our individual giftings to edify the body as a whole and our Father above.

Due to the very nature of man, disagreements will likely erupt among our congregations. Rather than creating an immediate recipe for dissension and division, these disruptions can allow our Father to bring conviction, redirection, and a tender heart willing to truly hear His instructions. As we strive to adhere to the path He has paved, Biblical principles of conflict resolution allow a glimpse of His nature and open the pathways for the Holy Spirit to work within us. So many of the misunderstandings and hurts prevalent within our congregations could be wiped away if we would only abide in our Heavenly Father and the commands He has graciously extended for our

[1] Michael Schiffmann, Return of the Remnant, 48.

prosperity.

A beautiful illustration of the precepts wrapped within a covenant can be found within a core Hebrew prayer, the Shema, or Sh'ma. As the central prayer in a Jewish prayer book, the Sh'ma is often the first section of Scripture memorized by a child. It is recited each morning and evening, as well as on Shabbat and special occasions. Comprised of three Biblical passages, the Sh'ma affirms God's chosen nation and calls to remembrance the covenant offered. When reciting the passages which follow, it is customary to cover the eyes so as not to be distracted by the things of this world.

The first section of the Sh'ma is comprised of Deuteronomy 6:4-9. "Hear, O Israel: the Lord our God, the Lord is one. You shall love the Lord your God with all your heart and with all your soul and with all your might. And these words that I command you today shall be on your heart. You shall teach them diligently to your children, and shall talk of them when you sit in your house, and when you walk by the way, and when you lie down, and when you rise. You shall bind them as a sign on your hand, and they shall be as frontlets between your eyes. You shall write them on the doorposts of your house and on your gates." Deuteronomy 6:4-9 ESV.

The second part of the traditional prayer establishes the blessings for obedience and warns of the consequences for turning aside. Referred to as the Vehayah, this passage arises from Deuteronomy 11:13-21:

"And if you will indeed obey my commandments that I command you today, to love the Lord your God, and to serve him with all your heart and with all your soul, he will give the rain for your land in its season, the early rain and the later rain, that you may gather in your grain and your wine and your oil. And he will give grass in your fields for your livestock, and you shall eat and be full. Take care lest your heart be deceived, and you turn aside and serve other gods and worship them; then the anger of the Lord will be kindled against you, and he will shut up the heavens, so that there will be no rain, and the land will yield no fruit, and you will perish quickly off the good land that the Lord is giving you.

You shall therefore lay up these words of mine in your heart and in your soul, and you shall bind them as a sign on your hand, and they shall be as frontlets between your eyes. You shall teach them to your children, talking of them when you are sitting in your house, and when you are walking by the way, and when you lie down, and when you rise. You shall write them on the doorposts of your house and on your gates, that your days and the days of your children may be multiplied in the land that the Lord swore to your fathers to give them, as long as the heavens are above the earth."

The third section of the Sh'ma, the Vaiyomer, is comprised of Numbers 15: 37-41 which is a call for the Israelites to remember the commandments and faithfulness of God.[2]

"The Lord said to Moses, 'Speak to the people of Israel, and tell them to make tassels on the corners of their garments throughout their generations, and to put a cord of blue on the tassel of each corner. And it shall be a tassel for you to look at and remember all the commandments of the Lord, to do them, not to follow after your own heart and your own eyes, which you are inclined to whore after. So you shall remember and do all my commandments, and be holy to your God. I am the Lord your God, who brought you out of the land of Egypt to be your God: I am the Lord your God.'"

All aspects of a covenant are exemplified through these passages, as the relationship is established, the conditions of the arrangement are specified, and signs are provided to assure the remembrance of the agreement. Through the words of Scripture outlined in this age-old prayer of the Israelites, we are reminded that Israel is God's chosen nation, destined to be wholly unto the Lord through the institution of covenant offered by the Most High. The second passage serves as a clear reminder of the blessings of obedience as well as the consequences for turning aside from His commands. Within the third passage, we are provided with the signs which were to be worn by the Israelites to serve as reminders of God's commands and faithfulness to His people.

Moving forward into the New Testament, we are privileged

---

[2] Hebrew4christians.com, accessed 7/27/15.

to see Jesus enumerate these principles once again, as He answers questions regarding the greatest commandment.

"And one of the scribes came up and heard them disputing with one another, and seeing that he answered them well, asked him, 'Which commandment is the most important of all?' Jesus answered, 'The most important is, 'Hear, O Israel: The Lord our God, the Lord is one. And you shall love the Lord your God with all your heart and with all your soul and with all your mind and with all your strength.' The second is this: 'You shall love your neighbor as yourself.' There is no other commandment greater than these.'" Mark 12:28-31 ESV.

Longing for fellowship, our Father entreats us to love Him and those upon our earth, to etch His commands upon our souls so that we might truly love and obey. A covenant brings to mind mutual blessing, honor, and respect that endures throughout the generations of time. Such relationships are steadfast and unchanging, unwavering in times of trouble, and rejoicing in times of blessing. Inherent within the core of a covenant is the authentication of a relationship and the conditions necessary to assure that the relationship progresses along the intended path.

Returning to the passage in Deuteronomy 6, we find "And when the Lord your God brings you into the land that he swore to your fathers, to Abraham, to Isaac, and to Jacob, to give you –to great and good cities that you did not build, and houses full of all good things that you did not fill, and cisterns that you did not dig, and vineyards and olive trees that you did not plant – and when you eat and are full, then take care lest you forget the Lord, who brought you out of the land of Egypt, out of the house of slavery." Deuteronomy 6:10-15 ESV.

Understanding the very nature of man, God again called the people of Israel to remember His covenant and the corresponding faithfulness, goodness, and protection of the Creator of all. By envisioning the concepts enveloped within the covenant offered by our Heavenly Father to the Israelites, we are allowed a glimpse into the nature of God and a portrait of a Father with love unfathomable in pursuit of a wayward creation. Once again, we are called to remember a Father who has remained faithful since the breath of creation.

4

Biblical History of Covenant
Adam and Eve

Are we able to find covenant principles and a covenant-keeping God as far back as the beginning of time? Absolutely. Our Heavenly Father desires above all things an intimate relationship with the very creation to whom He exhaled the breath of life. Let us journey back to the Garden of Eden and explore more fully the path of demise which forever altered God's original covenant with His creation.

A covenant is defined by the Hebrew word *brit*. While this often connotes a cutting of the flesh which draws blood, the simplistic meaning of the word is covenant, an establishment and verification of a relationship.[3] We were all created by our Father with an innate desire to seek fulfilling relationships with our Creator and those within our lives. As our world has spiraled ever deeper into the clutches of sin, our need for boundaries and clarifications regarding our relationships has increased. While there was no sin, the need for guidelines was minimal. However, as mistrust and sin entered the world, our need for stipulations became a necessity and steadily increased in proportion with the sins existing in the world around. The law was provided not as a means of justification but rather as a means of revealing to us the impossibility of living a perfect life and of our need for a Savior. From the instant Satan suggested the initial mistrust of the very nature of God, our loving Father set into motion an intricate plan of redemption which would cost His very all.

The first example of a covenant relationship in Scripture can

---

[3] Asher Intrater, Covenant Relationships, 26.

be seen in God's original relationship with Adam. Although this arrangement does not clearly disclose a formal offer of covenant, the relationship is established upon covenantal principles. Because sin did not exist at the time of creation, a specific offer of covenant was not necessary. Once sin entered the picture, the harmony of the relationship was disrupted, requiring effort to re-establish that which was lost in the transgressions. The law is given for the lawbreaker, that he may know his fallibility and need for redemption. Physically walking and communing with God on a daily basis, Adam was privileged to dwell within absolute perfection. The entirety of that perfection hinged upon a single rule, a rule given by the Almighty with the hope that true, reciprocating love and trust would prevail against the freedom to choose otherwise.

Within the words of Genesis 1 we find:

"Then God said, 'Let us make man in our image, after our likeness. And let them have dominion over the fish of the sea and over the birds of the heavens and over the livestock and over all the earth and over every creeping thing that creeps on the earth.'

So God created man in his own image, in the image of God he created him; male and female he created them.

And God blessed them. And God said to them, 'Be fruitful and multiply and fill the earth and subdue it and have dominion over the fish of the sea and over the birds of the heavens and over every living thing that moves on the earth.'" Genesis 1:26-29 ESV.

Created in the very image of God, man was provided with his mission statement: to multiply, to subdue the earth, and to take dominion over all the creatures which inhabit the earth. Although he lived in paradise, he was given responsibility and commanded to work.

"then the Lord God formed the man of dust from the ground and breathed into his nostrils the breath of life, and man became a living creature. And the Lord God planted a garden in Eden, in the east, and there he put the man whom he had formed. And out of the ground the Lord God made to spring up every tree that is pleasant to the sight and good for food. The tree of life was in the midst of the garden, and the tree of the knowledge of good and evil … The Lord God took the man and put him in the garden of Eden to work it and keep it. And the Lord God commanded the man, saying, 'You may surely eat of every tree of the garden, but of the tree of the knowledge of good and evil you shall not eat, for in the day that you eat of it you shall surely die.'" Genesis 2:7-9, 15-17 ESV.

If we paused for a moment and let the words comprising these passages truly filter through our beings, we would be struck with the intentionality and care of a loving Father fashioning man in His likeness and then crafting specifically for him a perfect dwelling place where all of creation lived and thrived in harmony. Food was provided, peace was established, and pure fellowship with our Creator was present continually. Man was provided with the authority to rule over all that God had created and commanded to multiply and work the garden. In addition to our innate desire to live within relationships, we are also created to be fruitful, to work within the callings placed upon us by our Father.

With these instructions, the Lord provided man with one rule – not to eat of the tree of the knowledge of good and evil. Because the earth was devoid of sin, the establishment of additional rules was not necessary. However, because our Father abounds with love, one rule was mandatory, for without choice there is no true love. Man was created in the image of the Almighty, with the ability to think, to feel, and to choose. Desiring our love above all, God provided man with a choice which would exact from Him the ultimate cost. Although He could have easily fashioned man programed to follow His exact specifications and desires, our Heavenly Father wanted us to intentionally choose to love Him. God always provides us with an option; never does He force His will upon us. Envision the imperfect man searching carefully or designing an impeccable surprise for a loved one, devising an elaborate plan for the presentation, and then waiting with baited breath and exhilaration as the gift is delivered. Next, imagine the Creator of all, with absolutely no limitations, carefully crafting and designing a flawless environment for the prize of His creation. How much greater is the expression, care, and love abounding within the actions of our Maker. Desirous of fellowship above all, He created man in His image and placed him within an environment of perfection unimaginable, longing for His creation to willingly follow His leading out of a heart overflowing with love. In spite of the cost involved and the nature of man, God provided Adam with all he needed: a mission statement, instructions, and a single rule.

"Now the serpent was more crafty than any other beast of the field that the Lord God had made.

He said to the woman, Did God actually say, 'You shall not eat of any tree in the garden?' And the woman said to the serpent, 'We may eat of the fruit of the trees in the garden, but God said 'You shall not eat of the fruit of the tree that is in the midst of the garden, neither shall you touch it, lest you die.' But the serpent said to the woman, 'You will not surely die. For God knows that when you eat of it your eyes will be opened, and you will be like God, knowing good and evil.' So when the woman saw that the tree was good for food, and that it was a delight to the eyes, and that the tree was to be desired to make one wise, she took of its fruit and ate, and she also gave some to her husband who was with her, and he ate. Then the eyes of both were opened, and they knew that they were naked. And they sewed fig leaves together and made themselves loincloths."

Genesis 3:1-7 ESV.

Reviewing this passage through the eyes of our Father creates an apprehension which is almost palpable, as we observe man's inability to truly grasp the depth of devotion flowing forth from his Creator. God's flawless design and plan for all of creation enveloped Adam and Eve as they strolled through the Garden, unaware of the potential dangers woven amidst a crafty serpent, a single rule, and a will to choose. With his initial words, Satan immediately planted a seed of doubt in the mind of Eve, directing her to look at something which might be withheld rather than acknowledging the multitudes of blessings provided. Instantly, a minuscule seed of distrust was planted, creating the unwarranted suspicion that perhaps the Creator was keeping something pleasant from them and that perhaps He did not truly carry their best interests within His heart. Upon glancing at the tree, Eve determined that it was good for food, a delight to the eyes, and capable of providing wisdom. We must take care not to be deceived by our eyes, to remain diligent and purposeful in following that which we hear rather than that which is visible. Immediately, their eyes were opened and sin's crushing force was revealed, allowing shame to overcome with the recognition that they were naked. Wrapped within nakedness in the Old Testament were the concepts of weakness, humiliation, and need. Within a moment, Adam and Eve awoke to the sudden and unfamiliar awareness of humiliation, lacking, and a need to find cover. While they sought to immediately cover themselves physically, they were incapable of providing the true covering necessitated by their actions of disobedience.

"And the Lord God made for Adam and for his wife garments of skins and clothed them.

Then the Lord God said, 'Behold, the man has become like one of us in knowing good and evil. Now, lest he reach out his hand and take also of the tree of life and eat, and live forever ---' therefore the Lord God sent him out from the garden of Eden to work the ground from which he was taken. He drove out the man, and at the east of the garden of Eden he placed the cherubim and a flaming sword that turned every way to guard the way to the tree of life." Genesis 3:21-24 ESV.

Upon hearing the sound of the Lord walking in the garden, Adam and Eve were struck with the sudden awareness of fear and hid from their Creator, withdrawing from the very fellowship which had sustained their existence. Using their newly gained knowledge, they immediately devised a scheme to cover their transgressions through their own means. How quickly they turned from the ways of the Father to the wisdom of man as a means of bringing atonement. After assessing the situation and pronouncing the appropriate consequences, the Almighty instantly set into motion the means by which man could be reconciled with his Heavenly Father. In spite of the betrayal He must have felt and with full knowledge of the ultimate cost involved, the Creator of all stretched forth His hand and provided the covering necessary to remedy man's condition. Unable to bear the thought of man living apart from Him for eternity, He drove them out of the garden, removing the possibility that they could live forever in separation. An outpouring of love unfathomable flowed forth from the Father, as He protected man from his own desires and banished him from the garden. In recognition of man's sinful nature and the seed of distrust planted within his spirit, the Lord removed man from the temptation which could have caused an eternal severance. Immediately a plan was enacted which would bring redemption to a world unworthy and restore all which was lost in the fall, if man would only choose to follow Him and accept the gift of salvation offered through the blood of Jesus.

Within the single act of providing the skins of covering for Adam and Eve, we are allowed to glimpse a beautiful portrayal and foreshadowing of our Messiah. Although Adam and Eve immediately recognized the error of their ways and tried to remedy the situation, they were not able to accomplish the redemption which would be required. Their actions of disobedience would require the mighty hand of God to move on their behalf and provide the atonement necessary to restore the fellowship they had lost. Just as God killed the first innocent animal to cover the physical bodies of Adam and Eve, our Heavenly Father established the means through which future sins would find remission. In keeping with the principles of the relationship, the violation of the covenant by Adam and Eve required a consequence. With a heart abounding in devotion, our Heavenly Father loved man through his transgression and stretched forth to pave a path by which he might return.

As we glance forward to the New Covenant, we envision the perfect Lamb of God serving willingly as the complete and final sacrifice for our sins and the true redemption which only He could provide. As always, our Father lays before us a choice and waits patiently for us to love as He has loved, to recognize the depth of devotion wrapped within His care, and to realize our need for the redemption He so graciously offers. As in the garden, His will is never forced upon us, and we are open to accept the free gift offered to us through scarred hands. If we could truly grasp the heartbeat of our Father, our eyes would be opened to the One whose love is boundless and Who desires relationships with His creation above all. A thread as old as time itself weaves meticulously through centuries of humanity to find fulfillment and completion through the redeeming blood of Jesus and the re-establishment of relationships offered to all who choose to follow.

5

Biblical History of Covenant
Noah

"The Lord saw that the wickedness of man was great in the earth, and that every intention of the thoughts of his heart was evil continually. And the Lord was sorry that he had made man on the earth, and it grieved him to his heart. So the Lord God said, 'I will blot man whom I created from the face of the land, man and animals and creeping things and birds of the heavens, for I am sorry that I have made them.' But Noah found favor in the eyes of the Lord." Genesis 6: 5-8 ESV.

A glance at the times surrounding the life of Noah exposes a creation in rebellion and a people who had lost sight of their Creator. As mankind wandered further from their roots and faith, their Heavenly Father again stretched forth His loving hand in offer of covenant, longing to re-establish the relationship for which man was created. As the nature of man worsened, the stipulations comprising the covenant increased. Let us journey back to the book of Genesis, and inhale an age-old Bible passage within the context of a covenant, truly breathing in the yearning of a Father for His creation.

As He surveyed a world created through His very words and the pinnacle of creation designed to shine in His image, our Heavenly Father was grieved and full of sorrow at the state of humanity. How quickly had the initial seed of mistrust sprouted into total depravity, causing the Creator to tread ever so closely to utter destruction of all. However, in spite of disappointment unimaginable and loss which cut through the recesses of His very heart, the Almighty again offered to man the possibility of returning.

"Noah was a righteous man, blameless in his generation. Noah walked with God. And Noah had three sons, Shem, Ham, and Japheth." Genesis 6: 9-10 ESV. For the sake of the remnant, the Lord provided another chance. Although the Torah had not yet been provided in its entirety, Noah found favor in the eyes of the Lord and was counted as righteous. With the bite of forbidden fruit in the Garden of Eden, the eyes of man were opened to the knowledge of good and evil, and an innate sense was immediately placed within each person allowing for the discernment between these entities. This inherent sense comprises the righteous law of God outside of the written code and is known as the Moral Law. Among a people corrupt and an earth filled with violence, Noah walked with God and upheld His Moral Law.

"But I will establish my covenant with you, and you shall come into the ark, you, your sons, your wife, and your sons' wives with you." Genesis 6:18 ESV. With these words, the Creator of all approached His righteous servant and provided the opportunity to walk with Him as never before. Even though Noah was almost six hundred years old at the time, He recognized the voice of his Father and diligently began the work to which He had been called. With faith unshakeable, Noah continued to follow his Father's leading as he constructed a boat of massive proportions, gathered the animals requested, and entered the ark with his family to await the unknown. As the waters of the deep sprang forth and the phenomenon of rain fell for forty days and forty nights, the righteous remained sheltered within the covering provided by their Father. After prevailing upon the earth for 150 days, the water began to subside and disclosed an earth forever altered. "And all flesh died that moved on the earth, birds, livestock, beasts, all swarming creatures that swarm on the earth, and all mankind. Everything on the dry land in whose nostrils was the breath of life died." Genesis 7: 21-22 ESV.

Onto this desolate and unfamiliar scene stepped Noah and his family. As change swirled, Noah acknowledged the One who had remained steadfast throughout the storm, the One who had extinguished all other breath upon the earth but Who had carried him upon the rising waves. After building an altar and providing burnt offerings, "… the Lord smelled the pleasing aroma, the Lord said in his heart, 'I will never again curse the ground because of man, for the intentions of man's heart is evil from his youth. Neither will I ever again strike down every living creature as I have done.'" Genesis 8: 21 ESV. While recognizing evil intentions within the heart of man and with full knowledge of the continuance of sin, the Lord extended grace and a covenant to His creation.

Prior to the offer of covenant, the Lord established the conditions upon which the relationship would be established.

Because the clutch of sin was strong within the earth, additional laws were required to assure the proper progression of the relationship.

"And God blessed Noah and his sons and said to them, 'Be fruitful and multiply and fill the earth. The fear of you and the dread of you shall be upon every beast of the earth and upon every bird of the heavens, upon everything that creeps on the ground and all the fish of the sea. Into your hand they are delivered. Every moving thing that lives shall be food for you. And as I gave you the green plants, I give you everything. But you shall not eat flesh with its life, that is, its blood. And for your lifeblood I will require a reckoning: from every beast I will require it and from man. From his fellow man I will require a reckoning for the life of man. Whoever sheds the blood of man, by man shall his blood be shed, for God made man in his own image. And you, be fruitful and multiply, teem on the earth and multiply in it.'" Genesis 9: 1-7 ESV.

Within this passage, the four Noahic Covenant Laws are presented, providing the foundation upon which man's relationship with his Creator would be established.

Although man was now allowed every moving thing as food, he was not to partake of meat which still contained blood, as the blood was considered to be the life of animal. All men would be held accountable for violence, the shedding of blood, and the killing of other people.

Because we are created in the very image of God, the sanctity of human life must be upheld. Noah and his family were instructed to be fruitful and multiply. Woven within each of these laws is the thread of life. With breath, God spoke into existence all of creation and exhaled into man the foundation of life. As all of creation moved in accordance with the sustenance provided by God, the life crafted and supported by that breath would be protected above all. Held cupped within the hands of our Father, life granted would be shielded by the covering of His hands and laws provided with His breath. Although given as food, animals would not be consumed while any trace of their vitality remained, for the life of any living creature is held within its blood. As the prize of creation and the very vessel for His glory, man was created in the image of God, and the sanctity of his life would be of utmost importance. Just as we are warned against bringing harm or violence upon another, we are also instructed to allow the life given to flow forth and to be multiplied. Interlaced within each of these directives is the respect and honor of life, as it is protected and instructed to flourish.

"Then God said to Noah and to his sons with him, 'Behold, I establish my covenant with you and your offspring after you, and with every living creature that is with you, the birds, the livestock, and every beast of the earth with you, as many as came out of the ark; it is for every beast of the earth. I establish my covenant with you, that never again will all flesh be cut off by the waters of the flood, and never again shall there be a flood to destroy the earth.'" Genesis 9: 8-11 ESV.

"And God said, 'This is the sign of the covenant that I make between me and you and every living creature that is with you, for all future generations: I have set my bow in the cloud, and it shall be a sign of the covenant between me and the earth. When I bring clouds over the earth and the bow is seen in the clouds, I will remember my covenant that is between me and you and every living creature of all flesh. And the waters shall never again become a flood to destroy all flesh. When the bow is in the clouds, I will see it and remember the everlasting covenant between God and every living creature of all flesh that is on the earth.' God said to Noah, 'This is the sign of the covenant that I have established between me and all flesh that is on the earth.'" Genesis 9:12-17 ESV.

After the conditions of the covenant have been established, the Lord provides man with a sign and another call to remembrance. Woven throughout Scripture is the urging of our Father for his creation to recall His faithfulness, devotion, love, and power. Longing always for man to remember and knowing the ease with which we fall into forgetfulness, He lovingly provides signs to bring to memory His works and promises, for His love endures forever. After stepping onto a world completely foreign, Noah was greeted by God and offered a covenant, confirmation of a relationship which was initiated by the Creator of all. Following the laws establishing the boundaries, the Lord promised to never again destroy all living creatures with a flood. Mindful of the nature of man, He then created a rainbow to paint the sky with the glorious colors of His design and to illustrate His very nature.

Although Scripture clearly delineates the four Noahic Covenant Laws as being provided to Noah, Jewish tradition recounts seven Noachide Laws. While both sets of laws carry the name of Noah, they differ greatly in their content and intentions. The laws comprising the Noahic Covenant are enumerated clearly in Genesis 9 as a set of standards by which Noah and his family would live upon their newly found earth. Even though they bear the name of Noah, the seven Noachide Laws of Jewish tradition were compiled as a general list to which all descendants of Noah would universally be held accountable. The seven Noachide Laws encompass prohibitions against idolatry, murder, theft, sexual immorality, blasphemy, and eating the flesh of a live animal. An additional component requires the establishment of courts to allow legal recourse. The basis for each of these may be found within the book of Genesis and serve as a standard by which all men and nations are held accountable.

Traveling forward into the New Testament, we see traces of the Noachide Laws enveloped with the context of Acts 15, as the apostles searched for ways of bringing Jewish and Gentile believers together in fellowship. Known as the fellowship laws, four regulations were established by the apostles as minimum requirements for the Gentiles which would allow them to worship and fellowship with Jewish believers without causing them to be ceremonially unclean.

In a letter written by the Jerusalem Council to the Gentile believers in Antioch, we find: "For it has seemed good to the Holy Spirit and to us to lay on you no greater burden than these requirements: that you abstain from what has been sacrificed to idols, and from blood, and from what has been strangled, and from sexual immorality. If you keep yourself from these, you will do well. Farewell." Acts 15: 28-29 ESV. Adherence to these laws would allow the Gentile believers to be welcomed into the Jewish homes and synagogues without danger of Torah and cleanliness violations.

Longing for the restoration of fellowship envisioned with the origin of time, our Heavenly Father has pursued a creation made in His image but tainted with sin. As covenant was offered, He lovingly provided the means by which we may be faithful as well as accompanying signs revealing His boundless devotion. From man's experience with the tree of knowledge, we were given God's Moral Law as a basic knowledge of good and evil. As descendants of Noah, we have been given the Noahic Laws as a call to remember and honor the sanctity of life. As believers in Jesus, we have been give the fellowship laws of Acts 15 so that we may live in unity with all believers, as we are truly one body crafted in the image of our Father and called to remember

His covenants and promises.

6

Biblical History of Covenant
Abraham

Through the life of Abraham, we are able to envision perfectly the various types of covenant extended by God to His creation. Often viewed as the patriarch of the Jewish nation, Abraham lived a life upon the foundation of covenants. A thorough examination of his life reveals one who was familiar with each variation of covenant and who faithfully lived a life firmly rooted within the principles of this concept.

Traveling forward from the days of Noah, we once again encounter a humanity who has lost sight of their Creator and a loving Father who stretches forth His hand to preserve the remnant. Reminiscent of His call to Noah, the Almighty moved on behalf of His creation to select a man who had abided faithfully by His Moral Law and extended to him the offer of a covenant. Similar to Noah, we see in Abraham a man of righteousness, willing to walk steadily into the unknown despite the comforts of his life. Choosing what would be deemed illogical to most, Abraham determined instead to follow the leading of his Father. A willing servant stepped forth once again to a land and a call foreign to his experience. From Genesis 12: 1-3 ESV, we find:

"Now the Lord said to Abram, 'Go from your country and your kindred and your father's house to the land that I will show you. And I will make of you a great nation, and I will bless you and make your name great, so that you will be a blessing. I will bless those who bless you, and him who dishonors you I will curse, and in you all the families of the earth shall be blessed.'"

With this passage, we are introduced to one of the most recognized types of covenant, a conditional covenant. As the conditions of the relationship are established at the beginning, the blessings which accompany obedience are then communicated. Inherent in the words spoken to Abram was the understanding that if Abram was obedient in leaving his country, God would form his descendants into a great nation and pour forth blessings innumerable.

Following Abram's departure and obedience, the Lord reiterates His offer of covenant and elaborates upon the blessings which were to come. "The Lord said to Abram, after Lot had separated from him, 'Lift up your eyes and look from the place where you are, northward and southward and eastward and westward, for all the land that you see I will give to you and to your offspring forever. I will make your offspring as the dust of the earth, so that if one can count the dust of the earth, your offspring all can be counted. Arise, walk through the length and the breadth of the land, for I will give it to you.'" Genesis 13:14-17 ESV.

Although chosen specifically by the Almighty as the one through whom His covenant would flow, Abram remained childless for many years and needed additional assurance. "After these things the word of the Lord came to Abram in a vision: 'Fear not, Abram, I am your shield; your reward shall be very great.' But Abram said, 'O Lord God, what will you give me, for I continue childless and the heir of my house is Eliezer of Damascus?' And Abram said, 'Behold, you have given me no offspring, and a member of my household will be my heir.' And behold, the word of the Lord came to him: 'This man shall not be your heir, your very own son shall be your heir.' And he brought him outside and said, 'Look toward heaven and number the stars, if you are able to number them.' Then he said to him, 'So shall your offspring be.' And he believed the Lord, and he counted it to him as righteousness." Genesis 15: 1-6 ESV.

Even though Abram required additional assurance, he believed the Lord and was counted as righteous. This declaration of a covenant is what is known as a kingly grant and required only belief on the part of the recipient. No conditions were set forth, and no enumeration of blessings or consequences were stated. To receive this covenant, one must only believe. Once the belief has been manifest, the gift is provided. The sign of the covenant established by this kingly grant would be revealed later as the child Isaac.

Carried forward into the New Testament, we see another example of a kingly grant offered to all humanity through the redeeming blood of Jesus. Out of boundless love and grace unimaginable, our Heavenly Father has offered salvation to a world unworthy on the sole basis that we believe. No conditions are established on the front, and nothing is required except belief. With this belief come the additional grants of eternal life and the Holy Spirit. We are powerless to do anything to earn either of these gifts, but we must believe that God's words are true. While salvation cannot be earned and is a kingly grant offered to all, the covenantal promises extended by our Father are conditional. The basis of our salvation stands independent from any conditions other than belief. With the indwelling of the Holy Spirit, grace is provided which allows the illumination of our Savior and fruit borne for His kingdom.

Continuing in Genesis 15, we find the ongoing dialogue between Abram and the Almighty concerning the promised covenant:

"And he said to him, 'I am the Lord who brought you out from Ur of the Chaldeans to give you this land to possess.' But he said, 'O Lord God, how am I to know that I shall possess it?' He said to him, 'Bring me a heifer three years old, a female goat three years old, a ram three years old, a turtledove, and a young pigeon.' And he brought him all these, cut them in half, and laid each half over against the other. But he did not cut the birds in half. And when birds of prey came down on the carcasses, Abram drove them away.

As the sun was going down, a deep sleep fell on Abram. And behold, dreadful and great darkness fell upon him. Then the Lord said to Abram, 'Know for certain that your offspring will be sojourners in a land that is not theirs and will be servants there, and they will be afflicted for four hundred years. But I will bring judgment on the nation that they serve, and afterward they shall come out with great possessions. As for yourself, you shall go to your fathers in peace; you shall be buried in a good old age. And they shall come back here in the fourth generation, for the iniquity of the Amorites is not yet complete.'

When the sun had gone down and it was dark, behold, a smoking fire pot and a flaming torch passed between these pieces. On that day the Lord made a covenant with Abram, saying 'To your offspring I give this land, from the river of Egypt to the great river, the river Euphrates, the land of the Kenites, the Kenizzites, the Kadmonites, the Hittites, the Perizzites, the Rephaim, the Amorites, the Canaanites, the Girgashites and the Jebusites.'" Genesis 15: 7-21 ESV.

Speaking to his faithful servant, God foretold the affliction which would befall the Israelites, the miraculous deliverance which would unfold, and the promise of a nation which was to come. Out of a heart abounding with love and desirous of unwavering belief, God wished to bestow upon Abram a kingly grant in which the promised child would come in accordance with belief. Upon Abram's request for additional assurance, God lovingly reached out and also offered to Abram an inter-personal, or parity, covenant. Symbolized by the smoking fire pot and the flaming torch, God then passed through the pieces of the sacrifice and offered a covenant with different implications. As a covenant of mutual blessing and honor, an inter-personal covenant reflects a relationship in which nothing is withheld from the other party. Both parties fully acknowledge that the possessions of one rightly belong also to the other and that honor and vulnerability flow freely between the two. By passing through the pieces, it is understood that if either party broke the conditions of the covenant, what happened to the animals would also happen to them. Within this passage, we see the offer of covenant, the blessings which would flow from obedience, and the repercussions resulting from violations. The sign of the covenant would finally come as Isaac. Parity covenants may exist between us and God or us and each other. To allow Abram rest within His promises, the Creator of all placed Himself under the self-maledictory oath exemplified by the passing of the fire pot and the torch.

We see another example of a parity covenant in Genesis 21 when Abimelech approaches Abraham, "'God is with you in all that you do. Now therefore swear to me here by God that you will not deal falsely with me or with my descendants or with my posterity, but as I have dealt kindly with you, so you will deal with me and with the land where you have sojourned.' And Abraham said, 'I will swear.'" Genesis 21:22-24. Within this passage lies the foundation of a relationship between peoples, a relationship of mutual blessing and honor which would extend beyond the initial parties to include the descendants who followed. The idea of covenant was so engrained within their hearts and minds that these simple words spoke volumes beyond their expression and served as the foundation for a binding of nations which would last for years to come.

As the years passed and the promised child was not conceived, Sarai offered to Abram her female servant Hagar in an attempt to attain the unborn child and the blessings foretold. The heart of the Almighty must have been heavy with sorrow as He watched the events unfold and yearned for His creation to truly comprehend the extent of His devotion, love, and faithfulness. With patience unimaginable, the Lord approached Abram again and said, "'I am God Almighty; walk before me and be blameless, that I may make my covenant between me and you, and may multiply you greatly.' Then Abram fell on his face. And God said to him, 'Behold, my covenant is with you, and you shall be the father of a multitude of nations. No longer shall your name be called Abram, but your name shall be Abraham, for I have made you the father of a multitude of nations. I will make you exceedingly fruitful, and I will make you into nations, and kings shall come from you. And I will establish my covenant between me and you and your offspring after you throughout their generations for an everlasting covenant, to be God to you and to your offspring after you. And I will give to you and to your offspring after you the land of your sojournings, all the land of Canaan for an everlasting possession, and I will be their God.' And God said to Abraham, 'As for you, you shall keep my covenant, you and your offspring after you throughout their generations. This is my covenant, which you shall keep between

me and you and your offspring after you: Every male among you
shall be circumcised. Both he who is born in your house and
he who is bought with your money, shall surely be circumcised.
So shall my covenant be in your flesh an everlasting covenant.
Any uncircumcised male who is not circumcised in the flesh of
his foreskin shall be cut off from his people; he has broken my
covenant.'" Genesis 17:1-10, 13-14 ESV.

In spite of his wavering belief, Abraham was again
reminded of the Almighty's devotion and promises to
come. As the father of a multitude of nations, Abraham was
offered an everlasting covenant and the opportunity to belong
wholeheartedly to the Father of all. Chosen from among the
entirety of creation, Abraham would be the spiritual father of
nations, pointing all descendants to the true Father and His
boundless love. Within this passage, we find a covenant defined
by its conditions, blessings, consequences for disobedience, and
an additional sign which would bring to remembrance the terms
of the covenant. As the Lord instructed the Hebrew males to
be circumcised as a sign of His covenant, so He longs for us to
allow the circumcision of our hearts, bringing forth the ability to
love Him with all our hearts and souls.

"After these things God tested Abraham and said to him,
'Abraham!' And he said, 'Here I am.' He said, 'Take your son,
your only son Isaac whom you love, and go to the land of Moriah,
and offer him there as a burnt offering on one of the mountains

of which I shall tell you.'" Genesis 22:1-2 ESV. As the recipient of God's covenant, Abraham obeyed the Lord's instructions with full knowledge that Isaac would somehow not perish. Because he walked with God, Abraham stepped forth again into the unknown to follow a call deemed illogical to the world. With covenantal concepts embedded in his soul, Abraham obeyed. From the breath of creation and through His covenants with Adam and Noah, God had established the sanctity of life and would not therefore require a human sacrifice. In accordance with his covenant, Abraham rested in the assurance that a great nation would come through Isaac. Additionally, because he understood fully the terms of the parity covenant offered by his Father, Abraham would have immediately known that if God was requesting Abraham's son, God would one day provide His son as a sacrifice. What a beautiful foreshadowing of the salvation which would be offered to all through the sacrifice of Jesus. At the heart of a parity covenant is the understanding that what's mine is yours, and what's yours is mine. Total, complete, unimaginable love is extended to all through covenant.

Also displayed within the life of Abraham was the Suzerian Vassal covenant, an agreement of old initiated between ancient kings. While one king was normally stronger than the other, this covenant provided each nation with mutual blessings and honor. The kings involved would agree to join forces together in the enforcement of boundaries, returning of slaves, and protection, binding their nations together in times of prosperity and trouble.

We are allowed to glimpse traces of this covenant in Genesis 12, when the Lord promises to bless the nations which bless Israel and curse those who bring dishonor. Abraham was guaranteed victory as long as he remained under God's covenant. This type of covenant was also revealed through the relationship between Abraham and Lot, as Abraham immediately set forth to rescue Lot from the hands of Chedorlaomer. We see traces of this covenant later in Genesis, as the Lord preserves Lot from the destruction of Sodom and Gomorrah. "So it was that, when God destroyed the cities of the valley, God remembered Abraham and sent Lot out of the midst of the overthrow when he overthrew the cities in which Lot had lived." Genesis 19:29 ESV.

Through the life of Abraham, we are allowed a glimpse into the very heart of our Creator, as covenants provide the pathway leading to the fellowship for which we were designed. Meticulously and lovingly, He has carefully crafted templates for us to follow, watching, yearning, and waiting for us to truly believe and absorb the magnitude of His care. Regardless of whether the relationship is being offered through a conditional covenant, kingly grant, parity covenant, or suzerain vassal covenant, an underlying thread is interlaced which establishes and supports a relationship founded upon His impeccable design. A thorough review and pause allow the intricacies and intentionality of our Creator to be absorbed and begs us to remember.

Tapestry Of Roots: Threads Woven By The Master

7

Biblical History of Covenant
Isaac and Jacob

"And God said to Abraham, 'As for Sarai your wife, you shall not call her name Sarai, but Sarah shall be her name. I will bless her, and moreover, I will give you a son by her. I will bless her, and she shall become nations; kings of peoples shall come from her.' Then Abraham fell on his face and laughed and said to himself, 'Shall a child be born to a man who is a hundred years old? Shall Sarah, who is ninety years old, bear a child?' And Abraham said to God, 'Oh that Ishmael might live before you!' God said, 'No, but Sarah your wife shall bear you a son, and you shall call his name Isaac. I will establish my covenant with him as an everlasting covenant for his offspring after him.'" Genesis 17:15-20 ESV.

In spite of repeated affirmations and a life lived in accordance with the will of his Father, Abraham found himself an aged man of one hundred still waiting for the perfect timing of the Almighty. Although he tried to alter the timing by providing an alternative solution, Abraham continued to wait. At least thirteen years had passed since the birth of Ishmael, and still he waited. Finally, the Lord appeared before him as he sat beneath the oaks at Mamre and offered the words Abraham so longed to hear, "I will surely return to you about this time next year, and Sarah your wife shall have a son...." Genesis 18:10 ESV. Although doubt lurked at the edge of Sarah's spirit, elation must have overcome as she learned that the time was truly drawing near.

Finally, a devoted man of one hundred held within his arms the promised child and a nation which would forever carry the name and identity of the Father. Held within the arms of his earthly father, Isaac was the sign of God's covenant with Abraham and further evidence of the Father's faithfulness. As a child of Abraham, Isaac walked in the ways of his father and lived within the confines of covenant relationships. He was privileged to grow beneath the nurturing covering of Abraham for seventy-five years and the boundless love of his Heavenly Father for an eternity, walking steadily forward as an earthly embodiment of God's promises to come and evidence of His faithfulness and love through the ages.

When faced with an approaching famine, Isaac had the opportunity to step forward and follow the examples of faith passed down from his ancestors. Just as Noah and Abraham had been called to a land unfamiliar, Isaac also was instructed to follow God and sojourn in trust in the midst of a foreign land. "And the Lord appeared to him and said, 'Do not go down to Egypt; dwell in the land of which I shall tell you. Sojourn in this land, and I will be with you and will bless you, for to you and to your offspring I will give all these lands, and I will establish the oath that I swore to Abraham your father. I will multiply your offspring as the stars of heaven and will give to your offspring all these lands. And in your offspring all the nations of the earth shall be blessed, because Abraham obeyed my voice and kept my charge, my commandments, my statutes, and my laws.'"

Genesis 26: 2-5 ESV.

Within this passage, the long anticipated sign of the covenant became the recipient of God's promises, as the Creator of all again stretched forth and extended to man the offer of a covenant relationship. Just as Abraham had obeyed the voice of the Father, Isaac was reminded of the blessings which would flow from obedience and the multitudes which would carry his heritage. Blessings innumerable would spring forth with each step of obedience.

As Isaac stepped forward in the land of Gerar, the name of the Lord grew in the land and the king of the Philistines Abimelech approached with offer of a parity covenant. "They said, 'We see plainly that the Lord has been with you. So we said, let there be a sworn pact between us, and let us make a covenant with you, that you will do us no harm, just as we have not touched you and have done to you nothing but good and have sent you away in peace. You are now the blessed of the Lord.'" Genesis 26:28-29 ESV. As the glory and faithfulness of the Almighty carried the Israelites and shone forth in might and strength, Abimelech re-affirmed his previous covenant with Abraham and acknowledged the God of the Israelites.

Obedient and sensitive to the Lord's leading, Abraham allowed his Heavenly Father to provide the perfect wife for Isaac from among his people. A life lived in harmony with the very heart of God was coming to a close upon this earth, as the Lord breathed the next chapter of His story. What a journey Abraham had faithfully followed throughout his 175 years, as he sought, listened, and obeyed the leading of the Almighty. Desiring a wife for Isaac who would share in his heritage, Abraham sent his trusted servant to Nahor and waited as the Lord brought forth the wife of His choosing. At the age of 40, Isaac took Rebekah as his wife.

"And Isaac prayed to the Lord for his wife, because she was barren. And the Lord granted his prayer, and Rebekah his wife conceived. The children struggled together within her, and she said, 'If it is thus, why is this happening to me?' So she went to inquire of the Lord. And the Lord said to her, 'Two nations are in your womb, and two peoples from within you shall be divided; the one shall be stronger than the other, the older shall serve the younger.'" Genesis 25:21-23 ESV.

Within this passage, we see the faithfulness of Rebekah, as she seeks the Lord's understanding above the wisdom of man. The Lord's proclamation that the older would serve the younger allowed for the passage of the covenant relationship and blessing to flow through the younger twin. Strong within Jewish tradition and woven throughout the history of the early Israelites were the concepts of the birthright and the blessing. The birthright had greater economic implications, as it granted to the firstborn male a double portion of the estate as an inheritance. If a family consisted of three sons, the estate would have been divided into four sections with the firstborn receiving two of the portions. Engrained deeply within their lives, the birthright was seen as a privilege designated by the Lord which should not be altered. The blessing, on the other hand, was granted to the child chosen by the father to be the head of the family after his death. Although this honor normally was bestowed upon the firstborn, this wasn't always the case and was left to the discretion of the father. By approaching the Lord with her struggles, Rebekah was privileged to see the heart of the Father and allowed to understand His design for the continuance of His covenant and the establishment of nations to follow.

Just as they had wrestled within the womb of Rebekah, the twins would continue to struggle as they matured into men from whom vastly different nations would be born. While Esau became a skilled hunter and man of the field, Jacob was quiet and stayed around the tents. "Then Jacob gave Esau bread and lentil stew, and he ate and drank and rose and went his way. Thus Esau despised his birthright." Genesis 25:34 ESV. When Esau sold his birthright to Jacob for a bowl of stew, his contempt for the customs and heritage of his people was revealed, and the words spoken by the Lord began to blossom to fruition.

With the loss of the birthright, a seed of bitterness sprouted within the heart of Esau, branching forth from a willful decision to go against the customs of his people to satisfy a transient need. When Isaac blessed Jacob instead of Esau, anger burned within

Esau, and Jacob fled for his safety. The desires of Esau's heart were exposed, as his full wrath was ignited more as a result of losing his position as head of the family than losing the birthright and heritage of his fathers. Resting beneath a momentary decision was the catalyst which would bring to fulfillment the Lord's words and the birth of a nation previously unknown.

When the time arrived for Jacob to be married, Isaac called forth Jacob as his own father had done many years before and requested that Jacob not take a wife from the Canaanite women. Obedient to his father, Jacob arose and began the journey to Paddan-aram to inquire of a wife from Laban, Rebekah's brother. While resting in the midst of his journey, Jacob was presented with an exquisite dream in which a ladder ascended to heaven and the Lord spoke directly to him.

"And behold the Lord stood above it and said, 'I am the Lord, the God of Abraham your father and the God of Isaac. The land on which you lie I will give to you and to your offspring. Your offspring shall be like the dust of the earth, and you shall spread abroad to the west and to the east and to the north and to the south, and in you and your offspring shall all the families of the earth be blessed. Behold, I am with you wherever you go, and will bring you back to this land. For I will not leave you until I have done what I have promised you.'" Genesis 28: 13-15 ESV.

While the Creator of all stretched forth His hand in offer of an unconditional covenant, Jacob responded that the Lord would be his God if He kept the conditions outlined. What a patient, loving, and merciful God we serve. With the assurance of the passage of God's covenant which had flowed through Abraham and Isaac, Jacob continued his journey to the land of Haran and the house of Laban. While laboring seven years for each of Laban's daughters, Jacob prospered and served Laban faithfully. Following the marriages, Jacob continued to work for Laban an additional six years in spite of repeated transgressions on the part of his employer. Throughout this time, Jacob was blessed with many sons; six through Leah, two through the servant Bilhah, two through the servant Zilpah, and one with Rachel. After the birth of Rachel's son Joseph, the Lord directed Jacob to return to his kin and the land of his fathers. As the Father had promised, Jacob had been blessed immeasurably while in the employ of Laban and protected from the schemes devised by the one he served upon the earth. On account of Jacob, Laban had also been the recipient of untold earthly blessings, and he approached Jacob with offer of a covenant upon their departure, providing security to each that neither would harm the other.

Stepping forth once again upon a path lined with uncertainty and fear, Jacob obeyed the voice of his Heavenly Father and trusted in the promises uttered by the very breath of God.

"Please deliver me from the hand of my brother, from

the hand of Esau, for I fear him, that he may come and attack me, the mothers with the children. But you said, 'I will surely do you good, and make your offspring as the sand of the sea, which cannot be numbered for multitude.'" Genesis 32:11-12 ESV. Stepping forth in obedience into a situation unknown, Jacob called upon the God of Abraham and Isaac and asked for remembrance of the covenant previously offered. In answer, the Lord Himself appeared to Jacob in the form of a man, Yeshua (Jesus), and wrestled with him throughout the night. As the day dawned, Jacob held onto the man and requested his blessing before relenting.

"And he said to him, 'What is your name?' And he said, 'Jacob'. Then he said, 'Your name shall no longer be called Jacob, but Israel, for you have striven with God and with men, and have prevailed.' Then Jacob asked him, 'Please tell me your name.' But he said, 'Why is it that you ask my name?' And there he blessed him." Genesis 32: 27-29 ESV. Following a night of wrestling, Jacob was provided a new name, allowing for the Hebrew meaning to transform from *heel-catcher / supplanter* to *may God prevail*.[4] Ever faithful and devoted, the Creator of all appeared to his servant in a time of fear and confirmed His covenant and blessings which were to follow. With the change of his name, the Lord blessed Jacob with an ever-present reminder that God would prevail, in spite of circumstances or trials. If Jacob would walk in obedience and rest in the assurances provided through the covenant, blessings innumerable would

---

[4] Meaningofnames.com, accessed 8/16/15.

flow, and the Lord's purposes would be further revealed.

The Lord thereafter appeared to Jacob again and elaborated upon the covenant established with his forefathers and destined for continuance through him. "God appeared to Jacob again, when he came from Paddan-aram, and blessed him. And God said to him, 'Your name is Jacob, but Israel shall be your name.' So he called his name Israel. And God said to him, 'I am God Almighty. Be fruitful and multiply. A nation and a company of nations shall come from you, and kings shall come from your own body. The land that I gave to Abraham and Isaac I will give to you, and I will give the land to your offspring after you.'" Genesis 35:9-12 ESV.

Jacob returned to the land of his kin bearing the promises of the Almighty and eleven sons from whom would flow His chosen nation and a line of kings. With boundless love and unimagined faithfulness, the Father of the universe covered Jacob with blessings and called to remembrance the covenant established originally through Abraham and Isaac. To receive the promises enumerated, Jacob need only to be fruitful and multiply, to father the nation destined to be priests to a world in need and a light to all who walk upon the earth. Wishing always for us to remember His ways, promises, and devotion, our Heavenly Father waits patiently for us to respond to His call and walk in obedience.

8

Biblical History of Covenant
Judah Introduced

Returning to the days of old, we see an earthly mission drawing to a close, as the one who wrestled with God Himself prepared to enter the glory revealed many years prior. The one chosen to forever bear the name of God's chosen people called together his sons to bestow upon each blessings and prophecies which would prove faithful throughout the passage of time.

Jacob first called to himself Joseph, with his sons Manasseh and Ephraim, and blessed him in accordance with his faithfulness and deliverance of the family. Although sold into captivity, Joseph rose within Egypt to be second only to pharaoh, as the Lord meticulously wove together the plan which would ensure the deliverance of His people and the preservation of His remnant. Through Joseph, the Lord had allowed the surrounding nations to glimpse His inconceivable power, care, and provision for those who called upon His name. The nations watched, as the Lord began to unfold a plan of perfect design, weaving that which had been intended as evil into a beautiful and miraculous path of redemption. As promised throughout the ages, He longed to carry His people forward so that they might in turn bless the nations and world to come. As Joseph walked in faith, allowing the mighty hand of the Father to shine before all, he was recognized also by his earthly father Jacob and received blessings innumerable. While these blessings were in accordance with a life filled with obedience and faithfulness to the Father, they would not carry forward to Joseph's descendants.

"Joseph is a fruitful bough,

a fruitful bough by a spring;

his branches run over the wall.

The archers bitterly attacked him,

shot at him, and harassed him severely,

yet his bow remained unmoved;

his arms were made agile

by the hands of the Mighty One of Jacob

(from there is the Shepherd, the Stone of Israel),

by the God of your father who will help you,

by the Almighty who will bless you

with blessings of heaven above,

blessings of the deep that crouches beneath,

blessings of the breasts and of the womb.

The blessings of your father

are mighty beyond the blessings of my parents,

up to the bounties of the everlasting hills.

May they be on the head of Joseph,

and on the brow of him who was set apart from his brothers."

Genesis 49: 22-26 ESV.

While Joseph was rewarded for his faithfulness, the line of

covenant and promise bestowed upon future generations would flow through the line of Judah, as the Lord longed to bring redemption to a world overflowing with need. Within the words of Genesis 49, we find Jacob's blessing to Judah.

"Judah, your brothers shall praise you;

your hand shall be on the neck of your enemies;

your father's sons shall bow down before you.

Judah is a lion's cub;

from the prey, my son, you have gone up.

He stooped down; he crouched as a lion

and as a lioness; who dares rouse him?

The scepter shall not depart from Judah,

nor the ruler's staff from between his feet,

until tribute comes to him;

and to him shall be the obedience of the peoples.

Binding his foal to the vine

and his donkey's colt to the choice vine,

he has washed his garments in wine

and his vesture in the blood of grapes.

His eyes are darker than wine,

and his teeth whiter than milk" Genesis 49:8-12 ESV.

Within this passage, we are allowed a glimpse into the heart of the Father, as an intricate plan of restoration begins to unfold. With His breath, the Creator spoke into existence all that resides upon this earth and breathed life into the nostrils of man. With His breath, He spoke blessings and covenants, providing for us a design by which we might live in harmony with Him and with those along our paths. Weaving as a thread through the descendants of Abraham, His covenant passed seamlessly through Judah pointing to the One who would bring redemption to the world. Prior to Judah, we are allowed a glimpse of the covenant offers extended to each of the patriarchs. With regard to Judah, however, we are allowed confirmation of the covenant when observed primarily through passages relating to the Davidic Covenant.

Tapestry Of Roots: Threads Woven By The Master

9

Biblical History of Covenant
Moses

"Now there arose a new king over Egypt, who did not know Joseph. And he said to his people, 'Behold, the people of Israel are too many and too mighty for us. Come, let us deal shrewdly with them, lest they multiply, and if war breaks out, they join our enemies and fight against us and escape from the land,'" Exodus 1:8-10 ESV.

As promised to the patriarchs, the Lord had bestowed blessings innumerable upon the Israelites, strengthening and increasing their number as He wove together the nation created to bring light to the world. Through Joseph, the remnant had been preserved, as they were carried safely through a famine which had devastated the surrounding land. By the devoted hand of the Father, the family of Jacob had been preserved, gathered, and delivered to the nation of Egypt, the most powerful empire at the time.

And then, the loving Father allowed the Israelites to be commuted to captivity where they would endure hardships unimaginable and serve an earthly empire determined to destroy their very existence. Although at times difficult for us to envision, the purposes of our Creator find their existence always in our good and intended for His design. With a heart abounding in love, the Father allowed His people to endure a season of trial so that the nation He envisioned might be created, protected, and matured into a people who would ultimately carry His promise to the nations. Although the Israelites traveled to Egypt as a group of seventy, they emerged upon their deliverance as a nation to be with over two million, on the brink of fulfilling the plan envisioned by the Father from the beginning. Although hardships abounded throughout the Israelites' time in Egypt, the Lord was all the while working their deliverance, gently shaping and forming a nation which would know no end. As a small group, the Israelites were protected from impending attacks by the mighty power of Egypt, as they grew in strength and number in spite of the surrounding circumstances. Because they were shepherds, the Egyptians refused to intermarry, and the bloodline of the Israelites remained pure. As the people of Israel passed through the Red Sea after centuries of captivity, they emerged as a pure nation of two million ready to fulfill the distinctive destiny to which they had been called. Through this season of trial and the deliverance which would follow, the Almighty created for His people a redemption which would carry through the ages and be recounted as an example of His faithfulness and care. As the breath of life exhaled into a nation unique, His name was magnified throughout the surrounding land. While the Egyptians intended to constrain and control, the Father prospered the Israelites, once again turning what man intended as evil into a divine plan of redemption and blessing.

With an ever present eye, the Father observed as His treasured nation began to take shape. As the time for its delivery drew near, the Lord orchestrated the salvation of the one who would bring redemption to the new nation. A Hebrew baby was born at a perilous time, and a loving mother crafted a plan born of faith and hope to provide protection against all odds. Moving in accordance with His divine plan and perfect timing, the Father allowed the Hebrew infant to be drawn from the river by Pharaoh's daughter and raised for a time by his own mother. While the infant was named Moses by the Egyptian princess, his Hebrew name Moshe carried the meaning of *drawn*.

"When Israel was a child, I loved him, and out of Egypt I called my son." Hosea 11:1 ESV. While Moses would lead the Israelites out of Egypt and provide deliverance for the new nation, so also would Jesus be called from Egypt to provide salvation to the world. This passage from Hosea foreshadows the Messiah and is echoed in Matthew 2:13-15 ESV, "Now when they had departed, behold an angel of the Lord appeared to Joseph in a dream and said, 'Rise, take the child and his mother, and flee to Egypt, and remain there until I tell you, for Herod is about to search for the child, to destroy him.' And he rose and took the child and his mother by night and departed to Egypt and remained there until the death of Herod. This was to fulfill what the Lord had spoken by the prophet, 'Out of Egypt I called my son.'" Ever present behind the readily seen, the Lord remained, carefully weaving the thread of redemption which would intertwine through the ages. As Moses was rescued from a ruler intent on killing the Hebrew babies in Egypt, Jesus was also rescued from a king who sought His demise. While Egypt enslaved the Israelites during the days of Moses, it thereafter provided a refuge for the Messiah from which He also would later be called. Out of Egypt, the Almighty summoned the nation of Israel, beloved and crafted to bear His name to the nations.

"During those many days the king of Egypt died, and the people of Israel groaned because of their slavery and cried out for help. Their cry for rescue from slavery came up to God. And God heard their groaning, and God remembered his covenant with Abraham, with Isaac, and with Jacob. God saw the people of Israel – and God knew." Exodus 2: 23-25 ESV.

Onto this scene stepped the grown Moses from the tribe of Levi. Unknown to Moses at this time, the Levites would later be blessed to serve as priests for the nation of Israel because of their refusal to worship the golden calf. As God spoke to Moses from the burning bush, fear flooded the heart and mind of God's chosen vessel. Afraid to peer at the Almighty, Moses hid his face and pleaded that he was incapable of the mission to which he had been called. How would he, slow of speech and tongue, actually summon the trust of the Israelites and persuade the most powerful nation in the world to release the people of God?

"And the angel of the Lord appeared to him in a flame of fire out of the midst of a bush. He looked, and behold, the bush was burning, yet it was not consumed. And Moses said, 'I will turn aside to see this great sight, why the bush is not burned.' When the Lord saw that he turned aside to see, God called to him out of the bush, 'Moses, Moses!' And he said, 'Here I am.'

Then he said, 'Do not come near; take your sandals off your feet, for the place on which you are standing is holy ground.' And he said, 'I am the God of your father, the God of Abraham, the God of Isaac, and the God of Jacob.' And Moses hid his face, for he was afraid to look at God." Exodus 3:2-6 ESV.

Shining forth through the flames, the God of Abraham, Isaac, and Jacob introduced Himself to Moses. As flames flickered, a divine mission was revealed to a man unsure, as a miraculous deliverance commenced. Within the words of Revelation 2:18 ESV we are provided a description of Jesus which corresponds with the flames of the burning bush. "And to the angel of the church in Thyatira write: 'The words of the Son of God, who has eyes like a flame of fire, and whose feet are like burnished bronze.'" As Moses hid his face, a reflection of a loving Savior with eyes of fire can be seen, as He commissioned the one specifically chosen to breathe life and liberation to a treasured nation. As Moses' journey continued, he would walk with the Father as never before.

Struggling to find confirmation of his calling, Moses asked, " …. If I come to the people of Israel and say to them, 'The God of your fathers has sent me to you,' and they ask me, 'What is his name?' 'what shall I say to them?'

God said to Moses, 'I AM WHO I AM.' And he said, 'Say this to the people of Israel, I AM has sent me to you.'" Exodus 3:13-14 ESV.

With these words, the Almighty introduced Himself to Moses as the great I AM, the name which carried holiness inconceivable and honor unimaginable. The name of the Father was so sacred that it was later known only by the high priest and uttered once a year on Yom Kippur within the Holy of Holies. Prior to his commissioning, Moses knew God only as Elohim, signifying the Creator and Judge of the universe, or strong one. In relaying the name I AM, God revealed to Moses a more personal nature, one which denoted presence, surety, and a heart forever present within the midst of His people. God lovingly assured Moses and the Israelites that He remained their covenant God, that He was in their very presence despite their current struggles, and that He would remain forever faithful. He was there, longing for their presence and desiring for them to know on a personal level that He was their God, their provision, their protector, and their ultimate salvation. Traveling forward into the New Testament, we also see Jesus identified as I Am within John 8:58 ESV: "Jesus said to them, 'Truly, truly, I say to you, before Abraham was, I am.'"

"And the Lord said to Moses, 'When you go back to Egypt, see that you do before Pharaoh all the miracles that I have put in your power. But I will harden his heart, so that he will not let the people go. Then you shall say to Pharaoh, 'Thus says the Lord, Israel is my firstborn son, and I say to you, Let my son go that he may serve me. If you refuse to let him go, behold, I will kill your firstborn son.'" Exodus 4:21-23ESV.

Before even embarking upon his divine mission, Moses was granted a vision of the path on which he would tread. In spite of untold wonders and miracles, the heart of Pharaoh would be hardened by the Almighty so that His glory, strength, and power might spread throughout the land, bringing the pagan nations to a knowledge of Himself while strengthening the faith of the Israelites. As plagues would rage, the Lord's people were clearly set apart, as He continued to pour faith into the hearts of a people enslaved for four hundred years, assuring that they were indeed His and that He had heard their cry. Prior to stepping foot onto Egyptian soil, the Lord also provided Moses with the culmination of the disasters to come, warning Pharaoh that his firstborn son would be required should he refuse to grant the Israelites freedom.

"God spoke to Moses and said to him, 'I am the Lord. I appeared to Abraham, to Isaac, and to Jacob as God Almighty, but my name the Lord I did not make myself known to them. I also established my covenant with them to give them the land of Canaan, the land in which they lived as sojourners. Moreover, I have heard the groaning of the people of Israel whom the Egyptians hold as slaves, and I have remembered my covenant. Say therefore to the people of Israel, 'I am the Lord, and I will bring you out from under the burdens of the Egyptians, and I will deliver you from slavery to them, and I will redeem you with an outstretched arm and with great acts of judgment. I will take you to be my people, and I will be your God, and you shall know that I am the Lord your God, who has brought you out from under the burdens of the Egyptians, I will bring you into the land that I swore to give to Abraham, to Isaac, and to Jacob. I will give it to you for a possession. I am the Lord.' Moses spoke thus to the people of Israel, but they did not listen to Moses, because of their broken spirit and harsh slavery." Exodus 6:2-9.

Centuries of hardships under the yoke of another had caused the Israelites to question to Whom they ultimately belonged. With heaviness and broken spirits, the people struggled to envision the destiny to which they had been called. Through days of unending toil, they labored as the promise of the forefathers began to fade from memory. Although their vision was clouded by distress, the Heavenly Father was weaving together a plan of unbelievable redemption not only for themselves but for the entire world. As the hand of the Almighty moved, nations took notice and the Israelites once again began to see their calling as the beloved of the Lord. Strengthening His people through signs and wonders, the Lord breathed renewed life and purpose into a nation long enslaved yet destined to reach the world. With feet treading upon dry land through the midst of the Red Sea, the Israelites walked forward into their calling. They had been carefully crafted, protected, and strengthened by the Father, and they were now ready to emerge as a nation unique, capable of independence and self-protection. Lead personally by the Almighty through cloud and fire, the people who had been set apart were carried forth by the Father through the wilderness as the pathway for true redemption was laid.

After journeying for approximately three months, the Israelites came into the wilderness at Mt. Sinai and encamped before the mountain while Moses went to speak with the Lord. Calling to Moses from the mountain, the Lord said, "Thus you shall say to the house of Jacob, and tell the people of Israel: You yourselves have seen what I did to the Egyptians, and how I bore you on eagles' wings and brought you to myself. Now therefore, if you will indeed obey my voice and keep my covenant, you shall be my treasured possession among all peoples, for all the earth is mine; and you shall be to me a kingdom of priests and a holy nation. These are the words that you shall speak to the people of Israel. All the people answered together and said, 'All that the Lord has spoken we will do.'" Exodus 19:3-6, 8 ESV.

Stretching forth through the words of Moses, the Lord offered a conditional covenant for the first time to a group of people as a whole, a nation chosen specifically with His hand and treasured above all. Previously, the Father's offer of covenant had been extended only on an individual basis to Abraham, Isaac, Jacob, and the kingly line promise to Judah. The Almighty had carried the Israelites forth from the lands of their forefathers, through trial and captivity, and into a redemption which would forever serve as a reminder of the Father's faithfulness. Crafting them into a people with a specific destiny and calling which would bring His redemption to the nations, the Lord further revealed His desire to bless all through Abraham. His treasured possession would become a nation of priests created to facilitate the relationship between man and God envisioned from the breath of creation. They were destined to be a holy nation, illuminating His Lordship to the ends of the earth. In exchange for obedience, the Israelites would be a treasured possession, a kingdom of priests, and a holy nation.

Upon hearing of the acceptance of His covenant, the Lord spoke to Moses, "Behold, I am coming to you in a thick cloud, that the people may hear when I speak with you, and may also believe you forever." Exodus 19:9 ESV. With exhilaration, the Lord hastened to meet His people, to reveal even more of Himself, to physically be in their presence as never before. With trumpet blast, smoke, cloud, and trembling mountain, the covenant God revealed Himself through roars of thunder as He spoke to their earthly leader. Rather than responding with awe and reverence, the Israelites were later filled with fear at the presence of the very One who had orchestrated their deliverance.

When considering covenant, the name of Moses almost immediately springs to the forefront of our minds. Within the Mosaic Covenant, God sets forth the conditions upon which His covenant would be based along with the consequences for disobedience. Desiring relationship with His treasured nation, He provided the Israelites with the Law and the additional commandments which would ensure their welfare and the fulfillment of their destiny.

Within the words of Exodus, Leviticus, and Deuteronomy, we are privileged to witness the birth of a nation and the guidelines provided by a loving Father to allow its prosperity. Similar to a Suzerian-Vassal covenant of old, the King of all extended to the Israelites the gracious opportunity to live under the authority of the Almighty. In exchange for faith and obedience, God's chosen people would receive protection, sustenance, and blessings innumerable. For disobedience, trials, disasters, and punishments would follow. Contained within these passages, the Lord provides directions and commandments to influence every aspect of the Israelites' lives. In Exodus 20, we find the Ten Commandments, or Decalogue, which serve as a template for relating to God and others. As the Israelites emerged and began to grow into their destiny, God provided them with commands which would also govern the civil and ceremonial/religious aspects of their lives. Systems were established by which the Tabernacle would be constructed, the priesthood established, and a system of sacrifices prescribed to provide atonement for transgressions. Longing to reconcile that which separated man from Himself, the Lord provided a way for sacrifices and for a dwelling for Himself amongst His people. To ensure harmony between the tribes and nations, a system of justice was established for all.

As a nation newly formed and stepping forth upon a

path emblazoned by the Creator of all, the Israelites were set apart as a nation unique. With a mighty hand, the Father had released them from the bonds of captivity, carried them through the waters of renewal, and established them as a people destined to be a light and salvation to the world. Providing them with everything necessary to prosper and fulfill their calling, all He required of them was love and obedience.

Although current interpretations of the Mosaic Covenant have divided the various commandments into sections pertaining to the moral, ceremonial, and civil life of the Israelites, the Jewish people at the time saw the compilation as a whole, the entire Torah. The 613 laws provided by God were valued and treasured above all, as they contained an exclusive covenant and offer to walk with a Father who had selected them from among the nations. Provided by God as a means of showing the utter inability of man to fulfill the requirements of the Law, these mandates were to work within the hearts of the Israelites, revealing their fallibility and need for a savior. Weaving throughout time the need for redemption and the miraculous deliverance to follow, the Father provided a real-life example of what was destined for the world as a whole through the blood of Jesus. With a heart abounding with mercy, God then provided the Israelites with the means of atonement and reconciliation when they would inevitably fall. As a sign of His covenant, the Lord commanded that the Israelites keep the Sabbath. While circumcision remained a sign of the individual covenant as descendants of Abraham, the Sabbath would serve as a sign of their covenant as a nation.

"Now when all the people saw the thunder and the flashes of lightning and the sound of the trumpet and the mountain smoking, the people were afraid and trembled, and they stood far off and said to Moses, 'You speak to us, and we will listen; but do not let God speak to us, lest we die.'" Exodus 21:18-19 ESV.

How the Father must have grieved upon the utterance of these words, as the nation specifically created for His purpose willingly forfeited a facet of its relationship. After all He had carried them through, the Israelites had not yet fully grasped the concepts wrapped within their covenant or absorbed the boundless love and protection of their Father. They had miles to traverse, trials to overcome, and an unwavering hand to guide them, although they did not yet fully comprehend or know the depths of the Father. Strength, surety, and faithfulness unimaginable surrounded them as they traveled, yearning to be acknowledged within the depths of their spirits. The Almighty had led the Israelites with cloud and fire, but the very power which had brought deliverance also frightened to the extent that they declined the opportunity to hear from God directly. How the mighty heart of the Father must have broken, as He longed to abide with them in every sense. Today, we yearn, search, and seek His presence, struggling at times to find that all surpassing love. We are so thirsty and crave His presence, pursuing that which was so freely offered to the Israelites. Yet, in spite of the Israelites' indiscretions, the Father's love never failed and the memory of His covenant stood, as He remained forever near and eternally faithful.

10

Biblical History of Covenant Israel

"I am the Lord; 'I have called you in righteousness; I will take you by the hand and keep you; I will give you as a covenant for the people, a light for the nations, to open the eyes that are blind, to bring out the prisoners from the dungeon, from the prison those who sit in darkness. I am the Lord, that is my name; my glory I give to no other, nor my praise to carved idols.'" Isaiah 42: 6-8 ESV.

Years later, the words of Isaiah would ring through the land of Judah, reminding the Israelites of their divine mission and calling. Destined to be a covenant for the people and a light to the nations, the new nation under the guidance of Moses had miles to traverse before understanding the essence of their relationship with the Almighty. The path set before them, culminating in the ultimate deliverance offered to all, was likely too enormous for them to grasp or truly comprehend.

"You are standing today all of you before the Lord your God: the heads of your tribes, your elders, and your officers, all the men of Israel, your little ones, your wives, and the sojourner who is in your camp, from the one who chops your wood to the one who draws your water, so that you may enter into the sworn covenant of the Lord your God, which the Lord your God is making with you today, that he may establish you today as his people, and that he may be your God, as he promised you, and as he swore to your fathers, to Abraham, to Isaac, and to Jacob." Deut. 29:10-13 ESV.

After journeying forty years through the wilderness and walking with the Father as never before, Moses gathered the Israelites and reminded them of their covenant relationship with the Almighty. Although their travels must have seemed without end, the Father had supplied every need, residing forever near and guiding without cessation. Because those who began the journey over the age of twenty had now perished, the promise was re-introduced to those who would be the recipients, who had been privileged to tread daily under the protection of a loving Father and truly knew His heart on a level beyond any before. The Israelites entering the land of promise had been granted the privilege of walking with the Almighty as far as memory would allow, maturing under His protective wing and absorbing His essence, love, and care. They had walked with Him and knew Him with a depth beyond that of their ancestors. They had been lead from above by the Creator of all and upon this earth by one who had been chosen specifically for such a purpose and time. Moses served as an interpreter and mediator for the nation of Israel, just as Jesus would serve for the nations.

After 120 years upon this earth, the deliverer of God's chosen people would soon see in fullness the One who had provided for his salvation and the birth of a nation unique. To lead His people toward the fulfillment of their destiny, the Lord commissioned Joshua and said, "… Be strong and courageous, for you shall bring the people of Israel into the land that I swore to give to them. I will be with you." Deut. 31:23 ESV.

As Israel halted on the edge of the wilderness, the one who had brought their earthly deliverance prepared to join the Almighty. Suddenly, the Israelites found themselves without their beloved leader and under the earthly guidance of another. With a loving hand of protection, the Lord commissioned a new leader who would facilitate the next stage of a miraculous plan, bringing forward a nation destined to be a light to the world. Just as the Lord exalted Moses in the eyes of His people, He also elevated Joshua, orchestrating a deliverance unimaginable. As their ancestors had done many years prior, the Israelites once again stepped forth upon dry land through the midst of a body of water as their destiny was revealed. Under the guidance of Joshua, the Israelites crossed the Jordan River upon dry earth and entered the land which had been promised to their forefathers. Moving through acts of wonder and miracles inconceivable, the Lord confirmed His calling of Joshua, breathed renewed faith within the hearts of the Israelites, and caused the surrounding nations to pause with awe and respect of the God of Israel. In obedience to the covenant established with the Father, the Israelite men received the sign of circumcision after crossing the Jordan, fulfilling the directive which had not been completed throughout the wilderness. As the Father crafted and guided the new nation, He longed for them to remember all that was wrapped within His covenant.

When the Israelites emerged upon the plains of Jericho, the hearts of the surrounding nations were filled with fear as awareness of the God of Israel swept over the land. Faithful to His covenant, the Lord allowed victories and blessings to flow as the Israelites walked in obedience to His voice. However, when disobedience surfaced, His presence was removed until repentance and restitution was complete. The God of the Israelites shone forth as He orchestrated victories in unfathomable ways, guiding, protecting, and providing for His people. After victories at Jericho and Ai, Joshua built an altar to the Lord on Mount Ebal and summoned the nation of Israel to renew the covenant with the Father.

"And afterward he read all the words of the law, the blessing and the curse, according to all that is written in the Book of the Law. There was not a word of all that Moses commanded that Joshua did not read before all the assembly of Israel, and the women, and the little ones, and the sojourners who lived among them." Joshua 8: 34-35 ESV.

In the midst of a land unfamiliar, the Israelites stepped forward into their destiny, providing for all a sign of the all-encompassing power of the Almighty and shining as a light to the nations. They stood out among the peoples as a group set apart by the Father, marked and chosen specifically by Him for a divine mission and calling. As signs of their covenant relationship with the Father, they were given circumcision individually and provided with the Law and Sabbath to observe corporately.

111

"Remember the Sabbath day, to keep it holy. Six days you shall labor, and do all your work, but the seventh day is a Sabbath to the Lord your God. On it you shall not do any work, you, or your son, or your daughter, your male servant, or your female servant, or your livestock, or the sojourner who is within your gates. For in six days the Lord made heaven and earth, the sea, and all that is in them, and rested on the seventh day. Therefore the Lord blessed the Sabbath day and made it holy." Exodus 20: 8-11 ESV.

Wrapped within the Law provided to Moses, the Sabbath exemplified the creativity of the Father and established a natural order to the passing of days. Although at times easily overlooked by those outside of Judaism, the Sabbath served as a fundamental part of the covenant between God and the nation of Israel, as it established a day dedicated to the praise and remembrance of the Father. As the Israelites embarked upon their calling, the seven day cycle of work and rest set the new nation apart and served as a cycle of life unique only to the people of Israel. To this day, the Sabbath is celebrated each week as a memorial to the Israelites' deliverance from slavery as well as the Father's design of creation. According to the order established with the breath of conception, the cycle of a day within the Jewish calendar begins at sundown and continues to the following setting of the sun. As such, the beginning of the Sabbath is traditionally celebrated on Friday evening with a special meal, lighting of candles, and prayer, as the family prepares to consciously enter a special time set apart for the Lord. The Sabbath serves as an integral component of weekly life within Judaism, as renewal is infused within the minds and bodies of those who partake, and the blessings of the Father are remembered.

Desiring a heart of love, the Creator of all provided the Israelites with the Law which would allow them to fulfill their destiny and be a light to the surrounding nations. The chosen of God viewed the Law as good, provided by a loving Father to disclose the best possible means of walking in the fellowship and forgiveness of the One who had crafted them into a nation unique with a calling destined to reach the ends of the earth. The Israelites stepped forward in obedience with a vision unimaginable and a deliverance unbelievable to a world in desperate need. Their love of the Almighty would be displayed to all around by the keeping of His commandments.

A familiar theme within the lives of the Israelites was the call to remembrance, as the Lord yearned to write upon their hearts His undying devotion. Out of a heart abounding with love, He repeatedly entreated them to pause and remember, to search for that heart of obedience, to remember the days of old, the deliverances provided, the mercy extended, and the commandments which would confirm the love of His people. As another call to remembrance, the Lord instructed the Israelites to wear the Tzitzit, or the Fringes.

"The Lord said to Moses,   'Speak to the Israelites and

say to them: Throughout the generations to come you are to make tassels on the corners of your garments, with a blue cord on each tassel. You will have these tassels to look at and so you will remember all the commands of the Lord, that you may obey them and not prostitute yourselves by going after the lusts of your own hearts and eyes. Then you will remember to obey all My commands and will be consecrated to your God. I am the Lord your God' …" Numbers 15:37-41 ESV.

While this is most commonly seen today as a prayer shawl or Tallit, the Tzitzit (fringes) continues to serve as a reminder of the Israelites' unique relationship with the Father. The strings and knots comprising the fringes symbolize the 613 laws of the Torah and remind the Israelite of his commitment to the Lord. The essence of the Tallit is to call to remembrance the faithfulness and love of the Father, to remember to Whom authority belongs, and to reflect constantly upon all that is enveloped within a relationship with the Almighty.

As the Israelites entered the land promised to Abraham, Isaac, and Jacob, they emerged as a nation set apart and unlike any other. Carrying the signs of circumcision and the Sabbath, they were established as a distinct nation prepared to shine as the light envisioned by the Creator of all. The nations were filled with awe and fear of the Israelites' God, and they watched from near and afar as the mighty hand of the Lord moved on behalf of His chosen people. Within the words of Isaiah, we are constantly reminded of Israel's relationship with the Father and her divine calling to reach the world.

"Thus says the Lord: 'In a time of salvation I have helped you; I will keep you and give you as a covenant to the people, to establish the land, to apportion the desolate heritages, saying to the prisoners, 'Come out,' to those who are in darkness, 'Appear' ...'" Isaiah 49:8-9 ESV.

Weaving the thread of redemption to all, the Lord spoke through Isaiah as His purpose was revealed and the Messiah foretold; the original recipients of His covenant would in turn become a covenant offered to the nations. Centuries later, the words of Isaiah rang true as the disciples gathered with Jesus for the Passover meal. "And he took a cup, and when he had given thanks he gave it to them, saying, 'Drink of it, all of you, for this is my blood of the covenant, which is poured out for many for the forgiveness of sins.'" Matthew 26:27-28 ESV. Desiring freedom for the prisoners and release from the chains of sin, salvation would be brought to a world in need. The nation of Israel was crafted as a radiance to the world, illuminating the darkness and bringing salvation, release, and freedom unimaginable and offered only by Him. With open hand, the Lord stretched forth and presented His treasured nation in offer of covenant, complete with all that is enveloped within the concept. As a covenant can only be accepted by those to whom it has been offered, the Father prepared a way so that all might receive that which He so longs to impart; salvation and restoration of the relationship envisioned from the breath of creation remained always the goal. The nation of Israel was created to be a light to the world, a nation of priests exemplifying the love of the Father and illuminating the path of salvation provided through the blood of Jesus. Ever present, our Heavenly Father waits, yearning for us to grasp the covenant which cost His absolute all, yet is offered so freely. Entreating those in darkness to appear and those in chains to come out, He longs to set us free, to breathe into our nostrils the entirety of His covenant and watch as we walk in the victory which has already been won through the death and resurrection of Jesus. As His chosen people, the nation of Israel will remain, preserved as a remnant with a destiny of inconceivable proportions.

Once we pause and reflect upon the history of Israel, our hearts and minds are opened to the true devotion, care, and protection of a loving Father towards his offspring, a depth of devotion inconceivable to us. Far exceeding anything supplied by an earthly father, the Lord provides for His nation and those who have been called according to His name. A vision of pure, unblemished perfection emerges as we absorb the attributes of His character and dedication to the people destined to bring blessing to the nations. Through Israel, we have been blessed with the Torah, ethical and moral laws, and an example of relating to God as He envisioned. Within the instructions regarding the temple, priesthood, and sacrifices, we are introduced to our inability to uphold the Law and to our subsequent need for atonement. As we understand the precepts of a covenant, the intended functioning of relationships, and our inability to maintain a righteousness on our own, we are brought face to face with our need for redemption. Flowing throughout the world and the passage of time, the blessing promised to Abraham would find fulfillment in Jesus, as the offer of covenant was extended to all.

Spoken through the words of the prophet Ezra, another facet to the Lord's divine plan of redemption is unveiled. "From the days of our fathers to this day we have been in great guilt. And for our iniquities we, our kings, and our priests have been given into the hand of the kings of the lands, to the sword, to captivity, to plundering, and to utter shame, as it is today. But now for a brief moment favor has been shown by the Lord our God, to leave us a remnant and to give us a secure hold within his holy place, that our God may brighten our eyes and grant us a little reviving in our slavery. For we are slaves. Yet our God has not forsaken us in our slavery, but has extended to us his steadfast love before the kings of Persia, to grant us some reviving to set up the house of our God, to repair its ruins, and to give us protection in Judea and Jerusalem." Ezra 9: 7-9 ESV.

To consider that the nation of Israel has been rejected by God is to completely misunderstand the heart and nature of the Almighty. Just as He has woven throughout the ages a plan for redemption, so also has He intertwined a principle which resides at His very core: a remnant. While our Father is one of steadfastness, He is also one of boundless love and devotion always searching for the return of His people and the fellowship for which they were created. He has shown over and over again, his heart of mercy, of searching for a reason not to judge, for any possible excuse to pardon, forgive, and shower with blessing. He longs to walk with us daily, to be the One to whom we turn instantly in times of sorrow or joy, to be our very essence and reside within our hearts, souls, and minds. He longs for a heart of obedience out of love and a unity that cannot possibly be severed. While the nation of Israel has not yet fulfilled her destiny, she has not been rejected, for God has always been faithful to provide and plan a remnant, just as He has orchestrated the delivery of salvation to all. Redemption and remnant weave together to provide a tapestry of salvation offered to the nations.

Within the principle of a remnant, we are privileged to glimpse the very heart of our Father. Just as He has interlaced the concepts of covenant and redemption throughout the passage of time, so also has He woven the principle of a remnant through the ages. The Hebrew word for remnant is *sha'ar* or *sh'aireet*, meaning *to remain* or *the remainder of what is left.* In spite of wickedness and disobedience unimaginable, our loving Father has always provided a faithful few who remained firm in His truths. The devoted remnant has bridged the gap between the created and the Creator and stayed the mighty hand of judgment until the majority has turned to repentance. Through the remnant, the promises of God are maintained for the majority and safely tucked away until such a time as disobedience ceases and repentance emerges. With a heart abounding in unfathomable love, our Heavenly Father offers our forward paths, searching and longing for any possible way to withhold the judgment we so rightly deserve. His is a heart of salvation rather than judgment, of fellowship rather than distance, and of love rather than coercion. As long as a faithful few remain steadfast in His truths, His promises will be held. Truly understanding the heart of God is to know that His love for us knows no end, that He is ever present, yearning for fellowship and searching for reasons not to judge. Standing in the gap, the remnant intercedes for the disobedient majority until true repentance and restoration is realized. They have been carefully crafted and empowered by the Almighty for specific times and destinies so that lives might be saved and the perfect will of the Father accomplished. While standing firm within the swirls of a straying majority, the call of the remnant is most often met with trials and storms. Sacrificing earthly comfort and acceptance, the faithful fulfill their calling and present themselves as a sacrifice of sorts to allow for the salvation of multitudes and the retention of promises of old. Through their faithfulness, they allow the preservation of the whole and intercession for the disobedient. If we would pause and linger a moment upon this principle, a picture emerges of a man upon a cross, a crown of thorns upon His head, and suffering unimaginable to allow forgiveness to all. The threads of remnant, sacrifice, and redemption are intertwined as the tapestry of salvation is woven and offered to the multitudes. While evilness abounds and wicked intentions reign within the hearts of man, a devoted Father waits patiently and yearns always to redeem.

To first see the idea of a remnant preserved, we need only return to Genesis. Within Genesis chapters six through nine, we find the familiar account of Noah. As God stood forever faithful and near, He watched as evil devoured the hearts and inclinations of man, causing the pinnacle of creation to drift further and further from their Creator. With sorrow, He grieved as those crafted to reflect His image instead shone forth wickedness. Determined to destroy all He had made, He glanced further and found Noah, with whom He found favor. Throughout his life, Noah had been faithful and walked in obedience to the Father while being molded into his destiny as the deliverer of humanity. While the waters exploded forth with destruction, Noah and his family were preserved upon the ark. A faithful group of eight had been set aside as a remnant, a bridge by which mankind could repent, re-populate, and return to fellowship with the Father. Through the remnant of Noah's family, humanity had been spared from the utter destruction wrought by the Almighty.

If we travel a bit further into Genesis, we are again confronted with the evil inclinations of man, as the Lord prepared to destroy Sodom and Gomorrah. Within the account provided in Genesis 18-19, we see the man who would become the father of the God's chosen nation and deliver blessings untold to a world unworthy. Knowing truly the heart of the Father, Abraham interceded for any righteous who might be found within Sodom. "Then he said, 'Oh let not the Lord be angry, and I will speak again but this once. Suppose ten are found there.' He answered, 'For the sake of ten I will not destroy it.'" Genesis 18:32 ESV. Abraham had walked with the Father and knew His devotion within the core of his being. Imploring the true nature of God, he understood that the Lord desired above all to save rather than to judge. For the sake of a remnant of ten, the Lord was willing to allow the continued existence of a city filled with evil. When ten righteous were not found, the Lord remembered His covenant with Abraham and provided deliverance for Lot and his wife prior to raining sulphur and fire from the heavens. As Abraham walked forward in obedience to God's covenant, he understood fully all that was wrapped within his agreement and the remnant which would flow through time.

Ever present and orchestrating all according to His perfect will, the Almighty continued to weave together the redemption which would flow to the world, as He set into motion the birth of a nation. Through the life of Joseph, we are allowed a glimpse into the intricacies of His plan, as a favored son was sold into slavery. What Joseph's brothers intended as evil, the Lord redeemed and provided salvation for a people of seventy destined to carry His blessing to all. As Joseph remained faithful throughout trials and deceit, the Father was forever near, crafting a beautiful plan of salvation for what would become His treasured nation. Through the hand of Joseph, food was provided in the midst of a drought and a people were gathered and called to the land of Egypt in fulfillment of their destiny. Without the placement and position of Joseph at such a time, the ancient Israelites would most likely have perished. However, behind the scenes, the Creator of all was meticulously devising another remarkable deliverance as He began to unveil the depths of His covenant. A group of seventy had been called for such a time and place to stand as a remnant, staying judgment and maintaining His promise of blessing within the midst of a pagan world.

As time progressed, a pharaoh arose who was unfamiliar with Joseph, and the Lord again transformed the evil intentions of humanity into His perfect will and design. While the Israelites labored in bondage at the hands of the Egyptians, the Lord crafted His nation, preserving and multiplying His people until timing was complete. With wonders unimaginable and devotion abounding, the Father called Moses to provide the deliverance of a priceless nation as His name resounded throughout the land. In spite of countless miracles and the guiding presence of their Heavenly Father, the Israelites soon transgressed and reverted to the pagan influences prevalent throughout their captivity. As their earthly leader basked in the very presence of God, those who had just walked a miraculous delivery convinced Aaron to craft a golden calf that they might worship.

"And the Lord said to Moses, 'I have seen this people, and behold, it is a stiff-necked people. Now therefore let me alone, that my wrath may burn hot against them and I may consume them, in order that I may make a great nation of you.' But Moses implored the Lord his God and said, 'O Lord, why does your wrath burn hot against your people, whom you have brought out of the land of Egypt with great power and with a mighty hand? Why should the Egyptians say, 'With evil intent did he bring them out, to kill them in the mountains and to consume them from the face of the earth?' Turn from your burning anger and relent from this disaster against your people. Remember Abraham, Isaac, and Israel, your servants, to whom you swore by your counsel, and said to them, 'I will multiply your offspring as the stars of the heaven, and all this land that I have promised I will give to your offspring and they shall inherit it forever.' And the Lord relented from the disaster that he had spoken of bringing on his people." Exodus 32: 9-14 ESV.

With a heart desiring that none should perish, our Heavenly Father searches always for the few who have remained faithful, the few who are charged with maintaining the Father's promises and truth until the majority repents and returns to their walk with God. As Moses interceded for the Israelites, he stood within the chasm caused by their disobedience and provided the remnant by which they might be saved from destruction. Even though Israel was at the height of disobedience and had grieved the Father immeasurably, the Lord allowed His covenant to stand and the

123

people to continue because of the remnant found within Moses. If Israel was to have ever been rejected, it would have most likely been at this point, as they plunged treacherously into the abyss of disobedience and disregarded the visible, leading presence of the Almighty. For the sake of Moses, the mighty hand of judgment was stayed. As Moses was found faithful, Joshua also stood, and then also the Levites, who were thereafter awarded the priestly role as a result of their faithfulness. The remnant of one influenced another, who in turn provided courage for an entire tribe. While staying the hand of justice and maintaining the promises, the remnant expanded and brought more within its fold. Eventually, the majority will recognize the error of their ways and return to the loving arms of a Father who has yearned always for their love and fellowship.

As we travel forward in Israel's history, we see repeatedly a people who have missed the mark and broken their covenant with the Almighty. Held within the clutch of sin, the chosen of God had forgotten their loving Father and turned from His ways. A nation destined to be a light to the world had returned to idol worship and paganism, destroying the altars of the Lord and killing His prophets. As wickedness swirled, the Father watched and allowed His chosen to be commuted to captivity and exiled from the land of promise. In 1 Kings 19, we encounter the prophet Elijah hiding in a cave and crying out to the Lord in despair. "He said, 'I have been very jealous for the Lord, the God of hosts. For the people of Israel have forsaken your covenant, thrown down your altars, and killed your prophets with the sword, and I, even I only, am left, and they seek my like to take it away.'" I Kings 19:10 ESV. However, for the sake of His beloved and the promises foretold, a loving Father had prepared a remnant who would hold the hand of judgment and cradle the covenantal promises until Israel repented and returned. While desperation coursed through Elijah's veins, the Lord spoke in a low whisper and provided reassurance of the remnant. "Yet I will leave 7,000 in Israel, all the knees that have not bowed to Baal, and every mouth that has not kissed him." I Kings 19: 18 ESV. For such a time, a group of 7,000 had been prepared and called by the Almighty to preserve the nation of Israel.

The remnant serves as a bridge, a connection to the Father by which the multitudes might find deliverance and re-institution of their promises when they return. Just as God orchestrated a plan of salvation from the beginning of time, so also has He crafted a faithful remnant within each generation and story which will bring about the fullness of His plan. Traveling forward to the New Testament, we find Paul addressing the very issue which remains a source of division within the body of believers today.

"I ask, then, has God rejected his people? By no means! For I myself am an Israelite, a descendant of Abraham, a member of the tribe of Benjamin. God has not rejected his people whom he foreknew. Do you not know what the Scripture says of Elijah, how he appeals to God against Israel? 'Lord, they have killed your prophets, they have demolished your altars and I alone am left, and they seek my life.' But what is God's reply to him? 'I have kept for myself seven thousand men who have not bowed the knee to Baal.' So too at the present time there is a remnant, chosen by grace. ..... So I ask, did they stumble in order that they might fall? By no means! Rather through their trespass salvation has come to the Gentiles, so as to make Israel jealous. Now if their trespass means riches for the world, and if their failure means riches for the Gentiles, how much more will their full inclusion mean!" Romans 11: 1-5, 11-12 ESV.

"Lest you be wise in your own sight, I want you to understand this mystery, brothers: a partial hardening has come upon Israel, until the fullness of the Gentiles has come in. And in this way all Israel will be saved, as it is written, 'The Deliverer will come from Zion, he will banish ungodliness from Jacob'; 'and this will be my covenant with them when I take away their sins.' As regards the gospel, they are enemies of God for your sake. But as regards election, they are beloved for the sake of their forefathers. For the gift and the calling of God are irrevocable. For just as you were at one time disobedient to God but now have received mercy because of their disobedience, so they too have now been disobedient in order that by the mercy shown to you they also may now receive mercy. For God has consigned all to disobedience, that he may have mercy on all." Romans 11:25-32 ESV.

Wrapped within the words of Paul the mystery is unveiled, as the divine destinies of man are revealed. Although separate and distinct, Jew and Gentile who have accepted Jesus as their Messiah constitute the body of believers, united in faith and Kingdom principles as one people. Together we represent the remnant of the faithful, each with a specific purpose and calling which is irrevocable and established to bring about His purposes. We are held together as one body cupped within the protective and powerful hands of the Almighty. Our heavenly Father is One of surety and safety, ever present and unmoving throughout the storms of life. He is the same yesterday, today, and tomorrow, and His will does not fluctuate, falter, or change. Believers in Jesus, whether Jew or Gentile, have specific gifts and callings which have remained ever present and constant since the beginning of time. He is carefully weaving the thread of redemption through the ages as He longs to pour His mercy and boundless love upon all. As the Almighty, He is sovereign, choosing the time and to whom His covenant will be offered. He has chosen the nation of Israel to be His treasured people and the Gentiles to spur the Jews to jealousy and return. Each play a part together in bringing about His purposes and redemption to the world, as salvation was never intended to be extended only to the Jew.

"What shall we say, then? That Gentiles who did not pursue righteousness have attained it, that is a righteousness that is by faith; but that Israel who pursued a law that would lead to righteousness did not succeed in reaching that law. Why? Because they did not pursue it by faith, but as if it were based on works…. For, being ignorant of the righteousness of God, and seeking to establish their own, they did not submit to God's righteousness." Romans 9: 30-32, 10: 3 ESV.

Even though the Israelites were the chosen of God, they failed to fully understand the depths of His love or all that was enveloped within their covenant. While their journey was marked by disobedience and indiscretions, the Almighty remained firm behind the covenant extended to their forefathers. By providing the Law, God yearned for His people to know His heart, to see their fallibility and utter inability to maintain the requirements. He longed for a heart of complete and total love, for an obedience springing forth out of adoration and gratitude rather than obligation. Although the Israelites saw the Law as good, they became more focused upon the letter of the law than the true heart applications beneath the surface. In pursuing their own righteousness, they were blinded to the essence of the Law and the true righteousness of their Father.

Within the words of Isaiah, we are again reminded of Israel's unique relationship with the Father. "In that day the remnant of Israel and the survivors of the house of Jacob will no more lean on him who struck them, but will lean on the Lord, the Holy One of Israel, in truth. A remnant will return, the remnant of Jacob, to the mighty God. For though your people Israel be

---

as the sand of the sea, only a remnant will return ..." Isaiah 10: 20-22 ESV.

"I will recount the steadfast love of the Lord, the praises of the Lord, according to all that the Lord has granted us, and the great goodness to the house of Israel that he has granted them according to his compassion, according to the abundance of his steadfast love. For he said, 'Surely they are my people, children who will not deal falsely.' And he became their Savior. In all their affliction he was afflicted, and the angel of his presence saved them; in his love and in his pity he redeemed them; he lifted them up and carried them all the days of old. But they rebelled and grieved his Holy Spirit; therefore he turned to be their enemy, and himself fought against them. Then he remembered the days of old, of Moses and his people...." Isaiah 63: 7-11 ESV.

The Father will always remember. As time has traveled forward, Israel has remained God's chosen nation, selected for a specific purpose and destiny which only she can fill. Although Israel has largely walked in unfaithfulness and failed to accept Jesus as her Messiah, her covenant remains because of the faithful remnant within her midst. Devoted and unchanging, the Father will always provide a remnant. A God of surety presides, with intentions and plans carefully orchestrated from the beginning of time to bring salvation and restoration to the world. Because of His covenant and the committed remnant, Israel remains His beloved. Desiring that all would return to His side, the Father waits patiently, longing and searching always for a faithful few. With a heart abounding in devotion and mercy, the righteous hand of the Lord has been stayed and a remnant maintained with the charge of preserving the promises of old. The role crafted for the Jews was to be a nation of priests destined to take the Kingdom message to the world. The Gentiles would walk in their destiny by spurring the Jews to jealousy for their own priesthood. Without the combined effort of both, the nations will not come to salvation. Without the Jews, the offer of redemption would not have been extended, and without the Gentiles taking the gospel to the Jews, God's chosen nation would not experience deliverance or walk in their calling. Today, the remnant of Israel is found within the Messianic Jews, while the Gentile remnant resides among the Gentile Christians and New Covenant believers. United by faith in Jesus, the Messianic Jews and the New Covenant believers each have distinctive values and separate covenants. Although the Israelites are God's anointed and chosen, the Gentiles' position within His story shines just as importantly and distinctly. Every believer in Messiah, whether Jew or Gentile, has fulfilled the role of the remnant, allowing lives to be saved and a great deliverance preserved until such a time as the multitudes return.

At the very core of a remnant is the concept of substitution, someone who stands in the gap between an underserving humanity and a sovereign God. As an intercessor, the remnant pleads for the salvation of the majority and stays the hand of judgment while disobedience appears to flourish. In doing so, the remnant often sacrifices earthly comforts and conformity to stand for the truth which sustains their very beings. Pointing always to the Savior, the entirety of Scripture reveals the Father's unwarranted but ever present love while a plan of intricate proportions is woven. With scarred hands outstretched, Jesus offers redemption to a world unworthy. Upon the cross, we see the culmination of the Father's design pouring out the concepts of covenant and remnant. The principle of the remnant has also pointed to Jesus, Who now sits at the right hand of the Father interceding on our behalf. Deep within those scars, we see the One who has stood in the place of all, the One upon whom all transgressions have been placed, and the One who has poured out His absolute all so that we might live. By His blood, the righteous hand of judgment has been stayed and salvation offered to a world undeserving.

As we glance back at the entirety of history, we see a nation crafted with a specific calling and destiny who has repeatedly fallen and forgotten the purpose for which she was created. Although Israel has walked in disobedience and broken her covenant, she has never been permanently rejected because of the faithful remnant of Messianic Jews. So, too, have we all fallen short, lost in the evil transgressions of our hearts and the deceit which so easily entangles. Yet, thankfully, the Father has not permanently rejected us. His is a heart which yearns for all to know Him, to breathe and thrive within the fellowship for which we were created. Waiting, longing, hoping, He is always there ready to provide a way to return. Rather than searching for transgressions or reasons to judge, He instead seeks the one tiny thing by which judgment may be withheld and we may be forgiven. Aren't we thankful that He has extended mercy to us and brought salvation when it wasn't deserved?

Just as the Father doesn't permanently reject us when we walk in disobedience, He has not and will not reject Israel. Through the principles of remnant, substitution, and sacrifice, we are blessed with a glimpse into the very nature of God. Operating within the concepts of covenants, remnants, and justice, the Almighty has provided countless examples of His faithfulness throughout the passage of time. To understand His nature is to know that He abounds with love unfathomable, that He is unchanging and steadfast, and that His will is perfect and irrevocable. While His justice is sure, He always provides a way back through repentance. All of humanity has fallen, yet the Father has woven a beautiful plan of redemption throughout the ages by providing a path by which we may return. That is His heart. How can it be said that He has rejected Israel because of her disobedience when He has not rejected us for the same thing? Surely, we have done as wickedly. If we accept Christ's sacrifice as providing salvation for us, how can it be said that it has been removed from Israel? Standing behind the sacrifice of Jesus is the principle of a remnant, distinct yet closely intertwined in purpose and meaning. The gifts and callings of

Biblical History of Covenant • Israel

God are irrevocable, and there has been and always will be a faithful remnant within Israel.

A beautiful day radiates upon the horizon, a day when the believing remnants of Jew and Gentile work together and usher in a harvest immeasurable. A great and mighty deliverance is coming, peeking forth from the edge of the distance and bulging with anticipation. As the new dawn emerges, the Gentile remnant will provoke the Jews to jealousy for their God, spurring a return to the God of their forefathers and a renewed recognition of their calling. The Jewish people will burst forth in their anointing and walk in their complete destiny, fulfilling their priestly role envisioned from the beginning of time. When the nations gaze upon the vigor and truth overflowing from God's chosen people, the Gentiles will experience a revival with a magnitude unprecedented. What a beautiful day when the Father's remnants, who have been gathered and prepared from the corners of the earth, truly walk in their distinct callings and fulfill the purposes for which they were created. How the Father will rejoice when His tapestry of salvation covers all who long to feel His touch, when the true nature of His heart resonates within us, and when fellowship is restored as intended from the commencement of time.

133

Tapestry Of Roots: Threads Woven By The Master

11

A Thread of Heritage
Pidyon HaBen
(redemption of the firstborn son)

Central to the lives of the ancient Israelites was the ceremony known as Pidyon HaBen, redemption of the firstborn son. Although this rite of passage hails from God's protection of the Israelites during the days of Moses, it contains enduring relevancy as a call to remember our Father's faithfulness and His plan for redemption. With the spoken word, our Heavenly Father crafted the world into existence and provided a template for all to live and prosper within the precepts of covenants. Immediately following the fall of man into the clutch of sin, the Creator of all provided for our redemption, offering to restore the intimacy of His fellowship which had been forfeited. Once we absorb the concepts wrapped within the age-old celebration of Pidyon HaBen, the magnitude of our Father's love and the redemption woven through Scripture shines forth in amazing clarity.

"Consecrate to me all the firstborn. Whatever is the first to open the womb among the people of Israel, both of man and beast, is mine." Exodus 13:2 ESV. With these words, we are introduced to the idea that the firstborn would be dedicated to the Lord for service. Because the firstborn male of each family is to be consecrated to the Lord's work, the ceremony of Pidyon HaBen is the process by which the child is redeemed and released from his obligatory service with the offering of five shekels. The ceremony is conducted upon the 31st day of the boy's life, unless this date falls on a Sabbath. At the prescribed time, the father brings the son to a Kohen, or priest, who recites the traditional ceremony. Following the exchange of coins and subsequent blessings upon the child, the ceremony is complete and a celebration marking the redemption commences. Today, the local synagogue rabbi takes the place of the Kohen and the five shekels are symbolized with five silver coins or silver dollars. If the firstborn son is not redeemed in this manner, it is understood that he is being dedicated to the Lord for His service. The possibility of redemption, however, does not exist for the firstborn sons of a Kohen, as they are required to be priests.

If we travel back to history's beginning, we see a similar concept wrapped within the intrinsic value of first fruits introduced within the first four chapters of Genesis. As direct descendants of those who once walked in the very presence of God, Cain and Abel understood the concept of covenants within their very core and lived according to the principles established from the dawn of time. However, Cain soon fell victim to Satan's snare of deception, which sparked the questioning of God's directives.

"In the course of time, Cain brought to the Lord an offering of the fruit of the ground, and Abel also brought of the firstborn of his flock and of their fat portions. And the Lord had regard for Abel and his offering, but for Cain and his offering He had no regard" Genesis 4:3-5 ESV. Within the early pages of Scripture, the Lord reveals the significance of the firstborn as being set apart for God and further establishes His expectations with regard to sacrifices. As one reared within a covenant community and familiar with the specifications required of an offering, Cain's actions were not in accordance with God's design. Rather than reflecting an obedient or submissive heart, Cain's offering revealed an attitude of pride and independence which lead to a sacrifice of his own choosing.

Throughout the passage of time, we are confronted repeatedly with man attempting to usurp God's ultimate authority and live according to his own wisdom and desires. In spite of our repeated trajectory down paths unworthy, our Heavenly Father abounds in love and offers always an avenue to return to His fellowship and obedience. As the pages of our past traverse before eyes opened, an enduring love grows forever stronger as it stretches forth to a creation undeserving of such devotion.

Perhaps most obviously, the Pidyon HaBen illuminates God's protection of the Israelites during the times of Moses. The deliverance begins with these words from Exodus 2:24-25 ESV, "And God heard their groaning, and God remembered his covenant with Abraham, with Isaac, and with Jacob. God saw the people of Israel --- and God knew." Following these words, the Creator of all moved on behalf of His people and began to reveal a mighty plan designed for their deliverance. As He hardened Pharaoh's heart, he repeatedly covered the Israelites with a protective hand while pouring down plagues unimaginable upon the Egyptians. With each denial voiced by

Pharaoh, God's name spread throughout the nations while His faithfulness and devotion were made apparent to the Israelites. With the final plague involving the death of the firstborn sons, God provided protection for His people through the blood of a lamb covering the sides and top of the doors to the Israelites' homes. What a beautiful illustration of the coming salvation offered to all through the redemptive blood of Jesus.

Following the Israelites' deliverance from slavery, the Lord further established the process of the firstborn's redemption in Exodus 13:13-16 ESV, "Every firstborn of a donkey you shall redeem with a lamb, or if you will not redeem it you shall break its neck. Every firstborn of man among your sons you shall redeem. And when in time to come your son asks you, 'What does this mean?' you shall say to him, 'By a strong hand the Lord brought us out of Egypt, from the house of slavery. For when Pharaoh stubbornly refused to let us go, the Lord killed all the firstborn in the land of Egypt, both the firstborn of man and the firstborn of animals. Therefore I sacrifice to the Lord all the males that first open the womb, but all the firstborn of my sons I redeem.' It shall be as a mark on your hand or frontlets between your eyes, for by a strong hand the Lord brought us out of Egypt." Because God had redeemed the firstborn through the blood of the lamb, He was now entitled to the firstborn of Israel.

A recurrent theme throughout the lives of the Israelites was that of remembrance, remembrance of God's goodness, faithfulness, protection, and devotion to His chosen people. The feasts, festivals, and traditions of the Israelites are prescribed by God and illustrate His unending dedication to His people. Aware of our tendency to forget and to quickly slide into a sea of doubt, our Heavenly Father has repeatedly called upon His people to remember, to keep Him ever present in the forefront of their minds. How quickly we turn to self-reliance in times of plenty while falling into despair when worries abound. It is imperative that we know His words, commands, and deeds, within the core of our beings so that we might always remember His desires and walk in obedience.

Following their deliverance from slavery and in spite of miracles unimaginable, the Israelites questioned the wisdom of leaving their bondage and desired to return to their prior lives which revolved around pagan rituals and captivity. While Moses was in the very presence of God, our Father's chosen people were overcome with doubt and turned to the worship of a golden calf. After interceding for the Israelites and staying the righteous hand of God, Moses returned to the former captives and asked who among them was truly for God. The Levites gathered to the side of Moses and obediently carried out the punishment prescribed by God. Once the required actions had been completed, Moses had these words for the Levites who had remained faithful, "Today you have been ordained for the service of the Lord, each one at the cost of his brother, so that he might bestow a blessing upon you this day." Exodus 32:29

ESV. As in the Garden of Eden, the entrance of sin necessitated an alteration of God's initial design, and the Levites were thereafter set aside for the Lord's service as a blessing for their faithfulness. Because this incident occurred within such a short span of time following God's directions regarding the firstborn sons, we do not see a clear portrayal of the development of Pidyon HaBen. Previously, the firstborn sons were considered to be set aside for service to the Lord, and a family was able to redeem their son from service if they could afford the price of the redemption. After the incident with the golden calf, it appears that the ceremony of Pidyon HaBen continued primarily for the redemption of firstborn sons who were not of the tribe of Levi. Exceptions occurred at times, as in the case of Samuel, who was presented to the temple for service rather than being redeemed.

As we travel forward into the New Testament, we are allowed a glance into this sacred tradition through the actions of Mary and Joseph, as they brought Jesus to the temple for His redemption.

"And when the time came for their purification according to the Law of Moses, they brought him up to Jerusalem to present him to the Lord (as it is written in the Law of the Lord, 'Every male who first opens the womb shall be called holy to the Lord') and to offer a sacrifice according to what is said in the Law of the Lord, 'a pair of turtledoves, or two young pigeons.' Now there was a man in Jerusalem, whose name was Simeon, and this man was righteous and devout, waiting for the consolation of Israel, and the Holy Spirit was upon him. And it had been revealed to him by the Holy Spirit that he would not see death before he had seen the Lord's Christ. And he came in the Spirit into the temple, and when the parents brought in the child Jesus, to do for him according to the custom of the Law, he took him up in his arms and blessed God and said, 'Lord, now you are letting your servant depart in peace, according to your word; for my eyes have seen your salvation that you have prepared in the presence of all peoples, a light for revelation to the Gentiles, and for glory to your people Israel.'" Luke 2:22-32 ESV.

One day, this One who was redeemed, would provide redemption for the nations.

Within the core of Pidyon HaBen lies a call to remember the faithfulness of our Creator and to envision pure redemption displayed upon a much grander scale. Throughout the pages of history, our Father has repeatedly pursued a creation striving to assert its own independence and pride. A fallen humanity, desperate to realize its own potential, has repeatedly relied upon its own thoughts and questioned the motives of the Heavenly Father. Just as He delivered the Israelites from bondage in Egypt, He again redeemed them from their own desires and shortcomings with the golden calf, providing always a pathway of retreat into His loving arms. Glancing further into history, we see the perfect sacrifice of Jesus and the ultimate plan of redemption crafted from the beginning of time and offered to all. As the blood over the doors of the Israelites' homes provided for their safety and deliverance, so the blood of our Messiah washes over us, cleansing us and protecting us from that which we truly deserve.

Returning to our passage in Genesis 4:5-7, "So Cain was very angry, and his face fell. The Lord said to Cain, 'Why are you angry, and why has your face fallen? If you do well, will you not be accepted? And if you do not do well, sin is crouching at the door. Its desire is for you, but you must rule over it.'" Let us absorb the essence of these words, listening carefully to the instructions with the willingness to follow always His leading. Let us chose the ways of our Father in lieu of our own desires and thoughts. Let our thoughts be of Him, captive not to ourselves but instead to the One who has given His absolute all to bring the restoration He has envisioned. Let us be alert to the lion crouching at our door and learn to rely upon the power of the One who reigns victorious and yearns for His people to believe and walk as the conquerors we are destined to be. Let us recognize that we truly have been redeemed, that we have been bought at a price immeasurable, and that all of creation sings of His glory and redemption. Pidyon HaBen provides a vivid reminder of God's faithfulness and devotion as it intertwines threads of redemption woven throughout time. Let us remember.

Tapestry Of Roots: Threads Woven By The Master

12

Biblical History of Covenant
The Davidic Covenant

"And the Lord said to Samuel, 'Obey the voice of the people in all that they say to you, for they have not rejected you, but they have rejected me from being king over them. According to all the deeds that they have done, from the day I brought them up out of Egypt even to this day, forsaking me and serving other gods, so they are also doing to you. Now then, obey their voice; only you shall solemnly warn them and show them the ways of the king who shall reign over them.'

So Samuel told all the words of the Lord to the people who were asking for a king from him. He said, 'These will be the ways of the king who will reign over you: he will take your sons and appoint them to his chariots and to be his horsemen and to run before his chariots. And he will appoint for himself commanders of thousands and commanders of fifties, and some to plow his ground and to reap his harvest, and to make his implements of war and the equipment of his chariots. He will take your daughters to be perfumers and cooks and bakers. He will take the best of your fields and vineyards and olive orchards and give them to his servants. He will take the tenth of your grain and of your vineyards and give it to his officers and to his servants. He will take your male servants and female servants and the best of your young men and your donkeys, and put them to his work. He will take the tenth of your flocks, and you shall be his slaves. And in that day you will cry out because of your king, whom you have chosen for yourselves, but the Lord will not answer you in that day.'

But the people refused to obey the voice of Samuel. And they said 'No! But there shall be a king over us, that we also may be like all the nations, and that our king may judge us and go out before us and fight our battles.'" 1 Samuel 8:7-20 ESV.

How the Father must have grieved, as He beheld the hearts and inclinations of His chosen nation. The plan He had designed with the breath of creation had been spurned by the very people for whom it was created, as the nation carefully chosen and crafted failed to recognize their true King. While the people of Israel grew in number and might, defeating nations and conquering the land provided by the very hand of the Father, they began to clamor and cry out for an earthly king. After being delivered, molded, and crafted by the mighty hand of the Father to be a nation unique and a light to the world, the Israelites chose to give up a part of their uniqueness and desired instead to be similar to those around, walking under the guidance of a fallible earthly king instead of the unblemished and unfaltering love of the Father. How often have we also yearned to put aside our uniqueness and walk in the ways of the world, hiding the light which has been created within us? From a heart abounding with sadness, the Father provided what His people desired, knowing that their choice would lead to troubles unimaginable and a wandering from the purpose for which they were created. Although He desired to be their one and only king, their source for all guidance, comfort, provision, and protection, He stepped aside and allowed the misguided desires of their heart. Without a choice, true love does not exist, as devotion coerced is not love at all. Although He knows the consequences flowing from our errant choices, He loves enough to allow the decision, waiting patiently always for our return and submission abounding from a heart of obedience and desire for His will. How much easier our lives would be if we would walk always in obedience, choosing continuously His perfect path and treading with submission bounding from love rather than obligation. In accordance with the Israelites' desires, He chose and anointed Saul to be the first earthly king over His chosen nation. The people destined to be a covenant to the nations turned from the One who had brought deliverance unimaginable and chose enslavement to an earthly king.

After Saul was anointed king, Samuel again pleaded with the people of Israel, entreating them to the recall the Lord's faithfulness in the past. While the consequences resulting from disobedience were sure, the ever present love of the Father remained, waiting patiently for repentance which would allow redemption. As Samuel recounted their history, the Israelites realized they had sinned in asking for a king. "And Samuel said to the people, 'Do not be afraid; you have done all this evil. Yet do not turn aside from following the Lord, but serve the Lord with all your heart. And do not turn aside after empty things that cannot profit or deliver, for they are empty. For the Lord will not forsake his people, for his great name's sake, because it has pleased the Lord to make you a people for himself. Moreover, as for me, far be it from me that I should sin against the Lord by ceasing to pray for you, and I will instruct you in the good and the right way. Only fear the Lord and serve him faithfully with all your heart. For consider what great things he has done for you. But if you still do wickedly you shall be swept away, both you and your king.'" 1 Samuel 12:20-25 ESV.

As years passed, man's sinful nature began to usurp submission to the Almighty, and Saul struggled to walk in compliance. Desiring obedience flowing from choice, the Father waited and watched as the one He selected to be king chose to walk in his own authority rather than under the One from whom all was granted. Just as it pleased the Lord to create the nation of Israel as a people for Himself, so Saul was chosen to provide the earthly guidance for His people. As is always the case, Saul was allowed a choice, a choice upon which the destiny of a nation hinged. In accordance with his position, Saul was granted kingship, prosperity, and blessings innumerable which coincided with rules and consequences for transgressions. Wrapped within all was choice, the choice to walk in obedience to the Father or tread according to his own desires. When faced with a mounting army of Philistines and an escalating fear which scattered his own men, Saul proceeded in offering to the Lord rather than waiting for Samuel and proceeding under the protocol established by the Lord. "And Samuel said to Saul, 'You have done foolishly. You have not kept the command of the Lord your God, with which he commanded you. For then the Lord would have established your kingdom over Israel forever. But now your kingdom shall not continue. The Lord has sought out a man after his own heart, and the Lord has commanded him to be a prince over his people, because you have not kept what the Lord commanded you.'" 1 Samuel 13: 13-14 ESV.

As the seed of pride and self-reliance took hold within Saul, the fear of the Lord was uprooted and prior devotion forgotten. The wave of sin progressed, sweeping Saul along its crest. When the Lord delivered the Amalekites into Saul's hand, the mission was one of utter destruction, including man, woman, child, ox and sheep, camel and donkey. When victory was attained, however, Saul chose to instead spare the Amalekites' king and the best of the livestock. With this action and the underlying heart intent, the Lord was grieved. Once again, the Lord had crafted and prepared, breathed life and prosperity into his chosen, and provided him with the gift of choice which could bring deliverance or destruction. As Saul walked in his own authority, the wave increased. "The word of the Lord came to Samuel: 'I regret that I have made Saul king, for he has turned back from following me and has not performed my commandments.'" … I Samuel 15: 10-11 ESV. Echoing words spoken long before, the Father again regretted that which He had created. As Saul was swept away, a man after His own heart was sought to be the prince destined to bring His blessing to the nations. Because of the faithful remnant within Israel, the nation was not swept away with their king. Another miraculous redemption and blessings untold were waiting within the weathered hands of a shepherd.

Cautiously leading, protecting, and nurturing, a young shepherd of ruddy complexion and handsome appearance walked alongside his sheep. As David guided the animals, Samuel waited patiently, surveying the sons of Jesse and listening to the voice of the Father. When Samuel's gaze met the beautiful eyes of David, the Lord revealed the one chosen to guide a nation unique. A lowly shepherd, summoned to rise from pastures to palaces, from sheep to a people chosen specifically by the Almighty, stepped forward in faith to a future unknown. Carried within the hand of the Father, David walked in faith unshakeable, ushering deliverance from the taunts of Goliath and bringing peace to the troubled soul of Saul. With a heart beating as the Father's, David moved in obedience, waiting patiently for the Lord's timing and will. As the pulse brought life to his body, David journeyed from a trusted comforter to one pursued. One who had once dined within the presence of the king found himself hiding among caves as Saul sought his very life. Although opportunities for revenge presented, David listened to the breath of the Almighty, allowing His forgiveness, patience, and grace to course through his veins as he waited for the Lord's timing. At least fifteen years would pass between David's anointing and the time selected for the beginning of his reign. As David walked, breathed, and lived with the Father through times of joy and struggle, the Lord meticulously prepared His chosen vessel for a divine mission and calling. From the hands of a shepherd, blessings would flow, as the Lord chose a common man to fulfill a divine calling. Years later, blessings would again flow from the scarred hands of a common carpenter as true redemption was offered to the nations.

As David walked with the heart of his Father, a mighty man of valor emerged, and the nation of Israel grew in might and number. Nations bowed as the God of Israel showered blessing, prosperity, and power upon His people, creating a fear and reverence for the Almighty which spread throughout the surrounding nations. Upon David's shoulders was placed a destiny of staggering proportions, as the Father began to unveil further details enveloped within His promises to Abraham. A plan conceived with the beginning of time would find fulfillment in the lineage of David, as a kingdom without end was established and a Messiah promised.

"Now when the king lived in his house and the Lord had given him rest from all his surrounding enemies, the king said to Nathan the prophet, 'See now, I dwell in a house of cedar, but the ark of God dwells in a tent.' And Nathan said to the king, 'Go, do all that is in your heart, for the Lord is with you.'

But that same night the word of the Lord came to Nathan, 'Go and tell my servant David, 'Thus says the Lord: Would you build me a house to dwell in? I have not lived in a house since the day I brought up the people of Israel from Egypt to this day, but

I have been moving about in a tent for my dwelling. In all places where I have moved with all the people of Israel, did I speak a word with any of the judges of Israel, whom I commanded to shepherd my people Israel, saying, Why have you not built me a house of cedar? Now, therefore, thus you shall say to my servant David, 'Thus says the Lord of hosts, I took you from the pasture, from following the sheep, that you should be prince over my people Israel. And I have been with you wherever you went and have cut off all your enemies from before you. And I will make for you a great name, like the name of the great ones of the earth. And I will appoint a place for my people Israel and will plant them, so that they may dwell in their own place and be disturbed no more. And violent men shall afflict them no more, as formerly, from the time that I appointed judges over my people Israel. And I will give you rest from all your enemies. Moreover, the Lord declares to you that the Lord will make you a house. When your days are fulfilled and you lie down with your fathers, I will raise up your offspring after you, who shall come from your body, and I will establish his kingdom. He shall build a house for my name, and I will establish the throne of his kingdom forever. I will be to him a father, and he shall be to me a son. When he commits iniquity, I will discipline him with the rod of men, with the stripes of the sons of men, but my steadfast love will not depart from him, as I took it from Saul, whom I put away from before you. And your house and your kingdom shall be made sure forever before me. Your throne shall be established forever.'" 2 Samuel 7:1-17 ESV.

Within these words, the Father reveals another aspect of His design, a plan intricately orchestrated to bring blessing to the nations. While re-stating the promise of land and descendants, a new dimension is further explained, one which involves thrones, kingship, and eternity. Through Abraham, the nation of Israel would be established as God's beloved, and promises unimaginable would flow forth to the corners of the earth. Wrapped within the covenant and promises intertwined, a new root would be established, which would carry with it the reigning kingship and promised Messiah. Fulfilling the blessing bestowed upon Judah in Genesis 49, the direct line of the Messiah is unveiled, and we see the one through whom the scepter will pass. While the ruling aspect of the covenant had been foretold prior, the specific line through which it would flow had not been revealed as David.

Reflected upon most frequently by the prophets when speaking of the tribe of Judah, the Davidic Covenant stands as the last Old Testament covenant. Within the words of Nathan, an unconditional covenant was offered, one which carried promises everlasting and required nothing on the part of the recipient. The Creator of all stretched forth and offered promises of a great name, everlasting kingdom, and land based solely upon His faithfulness while placing no requirements upon David or Israel. Traveling through the ages, the thread of redemption and authority flows through the line of David, finding fulfillment in Christ. Through the line of David, the promised Messiah would be born, and salvation would be offered to a world unworthy. True to the words of old, Jesus will one day return to establish His kingdom forevermore.

Within the words spoken through Nathan, we find reaffirmation of the promises to the patriarchs relating to the land and a nation. A people carefully crafted into a nation now walked forward under the guidance of an earthly king chosen by the Father for a specific time and purpose. Emerging as a nation unique, the Israelites carried the mark of the Father, as nations were destroyed, prosperity bloomed, and the name of the Lord was proclaimed throughout the land. With a heart abounding in devotion, the Lord first spoke confirmation to David and revealed His nature of surety. He thereafter disclosed the primary focus of the Davidic Covenant, as He addressed the seed from David's own body which would reign upon the throne forevermore. Enveloped within the concept of David's offspring are the aspects of a house and dynasty, a kingdom and people, and a throne forever which is unconditional and points to Jesus. With open hand, the Father offered steadfast, unconditional love, ever present and all encompassing.

As a shepherd boy transitioned into a warrior king, the people selected specifically by God walked with the breath of their Father. After reigning forty years upon the earth, the temporal reign of David began to draw to a close. As David prepared to join his Heavenly Father, He summoned Solomon and commanded, "I am about to go the way of all the earth. Be strong, and show yourself a man and keep the charge of the Lord your God, walking in his ways and keeping his statutes, his commandments, his rules, and his testimonies, as it is written in the Law of Moses, that you may prosper in all that you do and wherever you turn, that the Lord may establish his word that he spoke concerning me, saying, 'If your sons pay close attention to their way, to walk before me in faithfulness with all their heart and with all their soul, you shall not lack a man on the throne of Israel.'" I Kings 2:2-4 ESV.

Although David's earthly journey was complete, his name and family would reside with God's chosen nation forevermore, for his kingship would know no end. As the one after God's own heart passed into glory, the kingdom of Israel was established in the hand of Solomon. The original group of seventy which had joined Joseph in Egypt had now multiplied into a great nation, which included approximately 1.5 million men of valor. As Solomon stepped obediently into his destiny, he beheld at his side a people too great to be numbered, and he requested of the Lord an understanding mind. Although granted wisdom unimaginable, as well as blessings and riches unprecedented, Solomon was later ensnared by the wiles of his wives. In spite of warnings and appearances from the Almighty, the heart of Solomon strayed from his true love. As Solomon walked in the ways of his father, blessing and prosperity flourished throughout the nation of Israel. When Solomon turned from the Lord, adversaries were raised.

"And the Lord was angry with Solomon, because his heart had turned away from the Lord, the God of Israel, who had appeared to him twice and had commanded him concerning this thing, that he should not go after other gods. But he did not keep what the Lord commanded. Therefore the Lord said to Solomon, 'Since this has been your practice and you have not kept my covenant and my statutes that I have commanded you, I will surely tear the kingdom from you and will give it to your servant. Yet for the sake of David your father I will not do it in your days, but I will tear it out of the hand of your son. However, I will not tear away all the kingdom, but I will give one tribe to your son, for the sake of David my servant and for the sake of Jerusalem that I have chosen.'" I Kings 9-13 ESV.

As the years progressed, the one to whom unbelievable wisdom had been granted turned from truth and relied instead upon his own desires. Although the Father's anger burned, the covenant was remembered and the promises of old sustained because of the faithful remnant within the midst. Consequences would flow from disobedience, but the kingdom would not be entirely destroyed. Upon the death of Solomon, adversaries were raised who would usher in the repercussions warned. As Jeroboam, the son of Nebat, walked through the countryside

157

surrounding Jerusalem, he encountered the prophet Ahijah.

"Then Ahijah laid hold of the new garment that was on him, and tore it into twelve pieces. And he said to Jeroboam, 'Take for yourself ten pieces, for thus says the Lord, the God of Israel, 'Behold, I am about to tear the kingdom from the hand of Solomon and will give you ten tribes (but he shall have one tribe, for the sake of my servant David and for the sake of Jerusalem, the city that I have chosen out of all the tribes of Israel), because they have forsaken me and worshiped the Ashtoreth the goddess of the Sidonians, Chemosh the god of Moab, and Milcom the god of the Ammonites, and they have not waked in my ways, doing what is right in my sight and keeping my statutes and my rules, as David his father did. Nevertheless, I will not take the whole kingdom out of his hand, but I will make him ruler all the days of his life, for the sake of David my servant whom I chose, who kept my commandments and my statutes. But I will take the kingdom out of his son's hand and will give it to you, ten tribes. Yet to his son I will give one tribe, that David my servant may always have a lamp before me in Jerusalem, the city where I have chosen to put my name. And I will take you and you shall reign over all that your soul desires, and you shall be king over Israel. And if you will listen to all that I command you, and will walk in my ways, and do what is right in my eyes by keeping my statues and my commandments, as David my servant did, I will be with you and will build you a sure house, as I built for David, and I will give Israel to you. And I will afflict the offspring of

David because of this, but not forever.'" I Kings 11:30-39 ESV.

Tucked within the words of Ahijah is the Father's principle of a remnant and the heart of a loving father searching to withhold a judgment rightly deserved. Patiently, an offer was again extended from the Creator longing for His people to truly understand the depth of His devotion and the covenant under which they lived. Because of the remnant and the covenant extended to David, the promises of kingship and a nation would remain while the mighty hand of total judgment was stayed. While the affliction would last for a season, it would not persist forevermore. A faithful Father watched from within their midst, longing for them to grasp His nature and respond with a heart of obedience. While the nation crafted by the Almighty was divided, the tribes of Judah and Benjamin served as a remnant for the whole, united as Judah under the rule of Solomon's son Rehoboam. As spoken by Ahijah, the remaining ten tribes followed as Israel under the guidance of Jeroboam. As God's chosen nation tread the divided path, they were met with periods of blessing and trials which corresponded with their hearts' intent and obedience. While they walked in the ways of the Father, peace and prosperity flowed. With the straying of their hearts, trials and tribulation ensued, as the Father watched and yearned for the relationship He envisioned with creation's breath.

"For to us a child is born, to us a son is given; and the government shall be upon his shoulder, and his name shall be called Wonderful Counselor, Mighty God, Everlasting Father, Prince of Peace. Of the increase of his government and of peace there will be no end, on the throne of David and over his kingdom, to establish it and uphold it with justice and with righteousness from this time forth and forevermore. The zeal of the Lord of hosts will do this." Isaiah 9: 6-7 ESV.

In accordance with His covenant, the Lord spoke through the prophet Isaiah and provided a glimpse of the glory to come. A child would be given to a world bursting with rebellion, a world who had forsaken her God and walked in accordance with her own desires. Although One of might and power, He would lay it down for the sake of all, bearing suffering unimaginable to bring salvation to those unworthy. Through His perfect blood, redemption would flow to the world and allow the restoration of fellowship with the Creator. A true king was coming bearing peace, righteousness, and justice inconceivable. One mighty yet full of peace, of earnest devotion and care, a counselor like none other, and an everlasting father would enter the earth with a mission conceived at the beginning of time. One from the throne of David would come to establish a kingship which would know no end. When the prophet Nathan spoke to David many years prior, the Davidic Covenant was introduced. Within the verses of Isaiah, we see fulfillment of the words spoken through Nathan as the Father weaves through His story the coming redemption.

Expressions of the prophet Jeremiah confirm the Davidic

Covenant and further weave the thread of redemption, as the promised Messiah and the Messianic age to come are foretold. "Behold, the days are coming, declares the Lord, when I will fulfill the promise I made to the house of Israel and the house of Judah. In those days and at that time I will cause a righteous Branch to spring up for David, and he shall execute justice and righteousness in the land. In those days Judah will be saved, and Jerusalem will dwell securely. And this is the name by which it will be called; 'The Lord is our righteousness.' For thus says the Lord: 'David shall never lack a man to sit on the throne of the house of Israel,'" Jeremiah 33:14-17 ESV.

"And the angel said to her, 'Do not be afraid, Mary, for you have found favor with God. And behold, you will conceive in your womb and bear a son, and you shall call his name Jesus. He will be great and will be called the Son of the Most High. And the Lord God will give to him the throne of his father David, and he will reign over the house of Jacob forever, and of his kingdom there will be no end.'" Luke 1: 30-33 ESV.

As Mary trembled, the Lord spoke through the angel Gabriel, disclosing a plan of miraculous proportions and a future unplanned. With faith and favor, Mary stepped forward into a destiny which must have been beyond her wildest dreams and woven only by the hand of the Father. Illogical and unknown, the path to which she had been called would require ironclad faith and a sacrifice of sorts, but it would allow the opportunity to know the Almighty as none before and to blaze a path unimaginable. Mary walked faithfully forward into uncharted territory with the promise of the Father beneath her feet. Wrapped within the words spoken by Gabriel, the promises foretold by Isaiah are remembered and the fulfillment of the Father's plan is delivered. The Son of the Most High, the promised Messiah, would be conceived within her own body and would one day offer salvation, reconciliation, and blessings to the nations. The throne of David would reign forevermore.

Weaving covenant, remnant, and redemption throughout time, the Father has exposed His nature and the very beating of His heart. Once we pause and reflect upon the entirety of His story, the intricacies of His plan are revealed and the mysteries of time unveiled. Within the core of His spirit lies the desire for relationship, for obedience abounding from true love, for a creation who truly grasps the heart of its Creator. If we would be obedient to remember, our spirits would awaken to the true intentionality and perfection of His plan. Every piece, event, and person, has been carefully selected and prepared to uncover the beating of His heart - a heart abounding in grace and mercy, a heart desiring that none should perish, a heart promising a Messiah through the line of David. As His story continued through the ages, the tales of the Old Testament prophets faded and centuries elapsed. Forever near and always observant, the Father spoke again to His people in accordance with the pattern He established throughout time. Longing for all to know Him,

He would again speak to His creation through a covenant; a new covenant would be offered to all through the blood of the Messiah, as salvation and blessing would flow to the nations at the cost of His absolute all. We must always remember and truly understand the depth of all that has been offered within the covenant extended.

Tapestry Of Roots: Threads Woven By The Master

164

13

Biblical History of Covenant
Judah Revisited

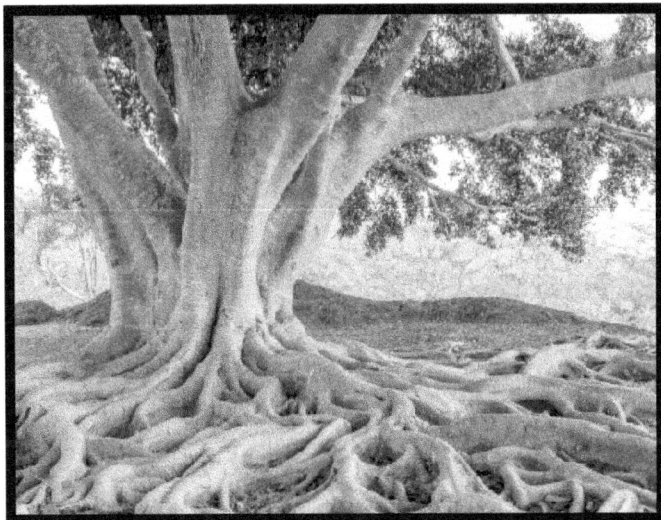

Prior to Judah, we are allowed a glimpse of the covenant offers extended to each of the patriarchs. With regard to Judah, however, we are allowed confirmation of the covenant when observed primarily through passages relating to the Davidic Covenant.

Through the eyes of the prophets, God's ultimate plan of redemption is revealed, as the promise of the Messiah and covenant are knit through the line of Judah. Spoken first through the words of Nathan to David, the covenant promise through the house of David is revealed and the promised Messiah foretold. Echoing the words spoken previously to Abraham, the Lord spoke to David and confirmed the same promises, ensuring a great name, land, and descendants from his own body which would carry the covenant. As the promise of covenant was to flow from Abraham's personal body, so also would the covenant issue forth through the seed and descendants of David's body, establishing a house and throne which would reign forevermore. The latter prophets continued to carry the thread of promise as the permanency of His kingdom was established through the tribe of Judah and the house of David.

Speaking to Nathan the prophet, the Lord states, "Now, therefore, thus you shall say to my servant David, 'Thus says the Lord of hosts, I took you from the pasture, from following the sheep, that you should be prince over my people Israel. And I have been with you wherever you went and have cut off all your enemies from before you. And I will make for you a great name, like the name of the great ones of the earth. And I will appoint a place for my people Israel and will plant them, so that they may dwell in their own place and be disturbed no more. And violent men shall afflict them no more, as formerly, from the time that I appointed judges over my people Israel. And I will give you rest from all your enemies. Moreover, the Lord declares to you that the Lord will make you a house. When your days are fulfilled and you lie down with your fathers, I will raise up your offspring after you, who shall come from your body, and I will establish his kingdom. He shall build a house for my name, and I will establish the throne of his kingdom forever. I will be to him a father, and he shall be to me a son. When he commits iniquity, I will discipline him with the rod of men, with the stripes of the sons of men, but my steadfast love will not depart from him, as I took it from Saul, whom I put away from before you. And your house and your kingdom shall be made sure forever before me. Your throne shall be established forever.'" 2 Samuel 7: 8-16 ESV.

The Lord thereafter appeared to David's son Solomon and confirmed the endurance of his kingdom. Within the verses of 2 Chronicles 7, we find, "And as for you, if you will walk before me as David your father walked, doing according to all that I have commanded you and keeping my statutes and my rules, then I will establish your royal throne, as I covenanted with David your father, saying, 'You shall not lack a man to rule

Israel.'" 2 Chronicles 7: 17-18 ESV. With a heart abounding in love, the Father reminded Solomon of his heritage and impending legacy while implying the conditions wrapped within the covenant. How He must have longed for His people to walk faithfully within the covenant offered and into the destiny for which they were created.

Flowing forth from a heart filled with compassion, the Lord later speaks through the prophet Isaiah, as He yearns for His people to listen, hear, and truly inhale the meaning of the covenant extended. Shining as a light to nations unknown, the people of Israel were destined to illuminate blessings innumerable and salvation to the world.

> "Incline your ear, and come to me;
>
> hear, that your soul may live;
>
> and I will make with you an everlasting covenant,
>
> my steadfast, sure love for David.
>
> Behold, I made him a witness to the peoples,
>
> a leader and commander for the peoples.
>
> Behold, you shall call a nation that you do not know,
>
> and a nation that did not know you shall run to you,
>
> because of the Lord your God, and of the Holy One of Israel,
>
> for he has glorified you." Isaiah 55: 3-5 ESV.

"Here I am." With the utterance of this impassioned plea, the heart of our Lord is laid bare as He cries out through the words of Isaiah, longing, yearning, entreating, so that He might in turn bring upon the nations the blessings He so longs to give. The design for worldwide redemption was further unveiled, although the rebellious heart of man continued to beat in accordance with his own desires.

"I was ready to be sought by those who did not ask for me;

I was ready to be found by those who did not seek me.

I said, "Here I am, here I am,"

to a nation that was not called by my name.

I spread out my hands all the day

to a rebellious people,

who walk in a way that is not good,

following their own devices;

a people who provoke me

to my face continually,

sacrificing in gardens

and making offerings on bricks;

who sit in tombs,

and spend the night in secret places;

who eat pig's flesh,

and broth of tainted meat is in their vessels;

who say, 'Keep to yourself,

do not come near me, for I am too holy for you.'"

Isaiah 65: 1-5 ESV.

The grief of our Heavenly Father is palpable, as He recounts the destructive ways of His creation and longs for the realization that He resides within their midst.   Spreading out His hands in offer of covenant, how He longs for all nations to find Him, to inhale His very essence and rest in the assurance of His promises.   Full of pride and independence, man has shunned the presence of the Almighty and relied instead upon his own wisdom.   Asking only that we seek and believe, He waits patiently as the thread of His story unwinds.   If only we would also be ready.

Through further words of promise, Isaiah again refers to the blessings which would flow to the nations. Reflective of the covenant to Abraham, Isaac, and Jacob, the Lord utilizes the words of Isaiah to recount the offspring promised to Jacob and the authority which would emerge from the tribe of Judah.

"Thus says the Lord:

As the new wine is found in the cluster,

and they say, 'Do not destroy it,

170

for there is a blessing in it,'

so I will do for my servants' sake,

and not destroy them all.

I will bring forth offspring from Jacob,

and from Judah possessors of my mountains;

my chosen shall possess it,

and my servants shall dwell there." Isaiah 65: 8-9 ESV.

Prophesying at a time concurrent with Isaiah, Micah was called forward with a message of admonition and restoration intended for the nation of Judah. Within the words of Micah, we find perhaps one of the most recognized passages foreshadowing the coming Messiah and His lineage through the tribe of Judah. The One from ancient days will come forth from the clan of Judah to bring restoration, peace, and security in the name of the Father.

" But you, O Bethlehem Ephrathah,

who are too little to be among the clans of Judah,

from you shall come forth for me

one who is to be ruler in Israel,

whose coming forth is from of old,

from ancient days.

Therefore he shall give them up until the time

when she who is in labor has given birth;

then the rest of his brothers shall return

to the people of Israel.

And he shall stand and shepherd his flock

in the strength of the Lord,

in the majesty of the name of the Lord his God.

And they shall dwell secure, for now he shall be great

to the ends of the earth.

And he shall be their peace." Micah 5: 2-5 ESV.

Approximately one hundred years after Micah, the Lord spoke through his prophet Jeremiah and provided further evidence of the redemption and Messiah to come. Although the nation of Israel had been divided and conquered by surrounding nations, the Lord was forever near. While repeated warnings of impending judgment issued forth from Jeremiah, he also delivered words of encouragement and promises of deliverance, as the Lord remembered His covenant and promises of old. Desiring His people to remember and call upon His name, the Lord promised to bring health, healing, prosperity, and security to the Israelites. The tribe of Judah and the lineage of David would forever reign upon the earth.

"Behold, the days are coming, declares the Lord, when I will fulfill the promise I made to the house of Israel and the house of Judah. In those days and at that time I will cause a righteous Branch to spring up for David, and he shall execute justice and righteousness in the land. In those days Judah will be saved, and Jerusalem will dwell securely. And this is the name by which it will be called: 'The Lord is our righteousness.'

For thus says the Lord: 'David shall never lack a man to sit on the throne of the house of Israel, and the Levitical priests shall never lack a man in my presence to offer burnt offerings, to burn grain offerings, and to make sacrifices forever.'" Jeremiah 33: 14-18 ESV.

As we travel forward another century from the days of Isaiah and Jeremiah, we are introduced to the prophet Zechariah, who brought forth a message of hope and encouragement. Having been allowed by King Cyrus in 538 BC to return to their land, the Israelites were in the process of rebuilding the temple when the Lord stretched forth, promising restoration for the nations of Judah and Israel.

"My anger is hot against the shepherds, and I will punish the leaders; for the Lord of hosts cares for his flock, the house of Judah, and will make them like his majestic steed in battle. From him shall come the cornerstone, from him the tent peg, from him the battle bow, from him every ruler – all of them together." Zechariah 10:3-4 ESV.

Within this passage, we are allowed to envision the covenantal line passing through Judah as the very Cornerstone is revealed. From the house of Judah would come the Messiah, the One who would provide the very foundation of Christianity, forever bind His people to their Creator, and Who would reign through eternity. Salvation would issue forth and the nations from every corner of the universe would be blessed as the Lord promised from the beginning of time. The lineage of that Cornerstone, when inspected and understood, carries with it promises unimaginable and complete restoration with the Creator of all, as He breathes love inconceivable upon a creation unworthy.

"And the surviving remnant of the house of Judah shall again take root downward and bear fruit upward. For out of Jerusalem shall go a remnant, and out of Mount Zion a band of survivors. The zeal of the Lord of hosts will do this." Isaiah 37:31-32 ESV.

Forever faithful, the Almighty again promises the preservation of a remnant through the house of Judah, a nation destined to carry His name through the ages. In honor of His covenant, He remembers, yearning for the nations to inhale His true essence and taste the redemption and blessings he longs to impart. He longs for the unveiling of our eyes so that we might glimpse the magnitude of His love, the intricacy of the plan woven from the beginning of time, and the covenants intertwined through the ages and offered to all through the blood of Jesus.

14

Breaking of Covenant

"Know therefore that the Lord your God is God, the faithful God who keeps covenant and steadfast love with those who love him and keep his commandments, to a thousand generations, and repays to their face those who hate him, by destroying them. He will not be slack with one who hates him. He will repay him to his face. You shall therefore be careful to do the commandment and the statutes and the rules that I command you today." Deut. 7:9-11 ESV.

Through the words of Moses, God's heart is laid bare. He is faithful, steadfast, and just, desiring that those chosen as His own would love Him and walk in obedience. Because the Father places such extreme value upon covenants, a high price must be exacted once a covenant is broken. While our Heavenly Father abounds with love and mercy, He is also One of justice, requiring repentance and atonement when His commands have been violated. As He watches, He yearns for us to grasp His devotion and care, to understand the pathway created by Him and offered to bring restoration. The Scriptures are replete with portrayals of humanity who have walked according to their own desires and forgotten the One who crafted their very beings. While disobedience has flourished, He has waited patiently, longing for all to return and searching always for the reason to spare the judgment deserved by His creation.

Following the thread to the beginning of time, we encounter Adam, created from the very breath of the Father and placed into a paradise where every need and desire was met. Included in the instructions to multiply and subdue the earth was a single rule, for in the absence of sin only one rule is necessary. Although Adam walked daily in the presence of the Father, the rule provided proved to be too great. A single rule, with repercussions inconceivable and upon which would hinge the very fate of humanity, was issued by the Almighty. With the breaking of this covenant, sin entered the world, forever separating man from his Father. As disharmony erupted and sin and death burst forth, Adam was banished from the garden. The breaking of the covenant was irrevocable, lasting throughout all of time, and requiring an atonement to allow reconciliation. Immediately, the Father put in place His plan for restoration, covering Adam and Eve with the atonement necessary to restore the fellowship for which they were created.[5]

Traveling forward in history, a loving Father surveyed a creation fashioned with His very breath but no longer sustained by the exhalation which had once brought life. As His mighty heart grieved, He contemplated the destruction of all He had meticulously crafted. The heart of man no longer beat in time to His own but was instead filled with every inclination of evil. With man's first betrayal and the entrance of sin, the righteous law of God was placed within each person, allowing for the discernment between good and evil. Although not a specific covenant, this inherent Moral Law required man to walk in accordance with what he knew as good and righteous. For choosing to proceed

---

[5] Gensis 1-3.

according to his own desires and walking in the ways of evil, consequences were still to be found. As sorrow flowed forth, the Father searched for a reason not to bring utter judgment upon all, for the remnant through which His hope and promises could be maintained. As His gaze encompassed the earth, His eyes rested upon Noah with whom He had found favor. While wickedness devoured the hearts of man, Noah had walked with the Father, remaining steadfast, righteous, and blameless. While man's disobedience brought forth destruction, the faithfulness of Noah provided the remnant. With the family of Noah, the Father's hope was maintained and a new beginning offered. As Noah's family stepped from the ark into a world unknown, the Father stretched forth in offer of covenant, providing additional laws to ensure their relationship and a sign by which His faithfulness would be remembered.[6]

As time wove through history, the resulting tapestry darkened as the clutch of sin gained a greater hold. While evil flourished, the Father was forever near, longing for His creation to remember, to walk in an obedience pouring forth from a love purely devoted. As transgressions worsened, more rules were provided so that eyes might be opened to fallibility and a need for redemption. Throughout the book of Deuteronomy, we encounter an obedient servant struggling to breathe into a treasured nation the true calling and uniqueness of its existence. As Moses gathered the Israelites, he recounted their cherished status, miraculous delivery, and their sustenance through the

---

[6] Genesis 6-9.

journey while he entreated them to remember all. Through his words, the Lord provided the entirety of the Law, which would govern every aspect of the Israelites' lives. When they walked in obedience, blessings abounded. For unbelief and grumbling, chastisement ensued. Although they had walked with the Father as none before, their failure to truly grasp the power of the Almighty and to remember His faithfulness prohibited all but two of the original travelers from entering the land of Promise. When they walked in accordance with His leading, nations were brought to their feet. As they attempted to proceed on their own strength and wisdom, the surrounding nations prevailed.

Within the words of Deuteronomy 28, the Lord outlined the conditions of the covenant extended to the Israelites, as Moses relayed the blessings flowing forth from obedience and the curses resulting from indiscretions. "The Lord will send on you curses, confusion, and frustration in all that you undertake to do, until you are destroyed and perish quickly on account of the evil of your deeds, because you have forsaken me." Deut. 28:20 ESV. Confusion and frustration would supplant the peace and sustenance provided by the Father. Curses, disease, and drought would devour the land and people as they struggled to walk in accordance with own hearts rather than the beating of their Redeemer's. While they toiled and labored to survive, their work would return void, and their efforts would be in vain. As they suffered defeat and oppression at the hands of their enemies, the surrounding nations would respond, "… It is because they abandoned the covenant of the Lord, the god of their fathers, which he made with them when he brought them out of the land of Egypt, and went and served other gods and worshiped them, gods whom they had not known and whom he had not allotted to them. Therefore the anger of the Lord was kindled against this land, bringing upon it all the curses written in this book, and the Lord uprooted them from their land in anger and fury and great wrath, and cast them into another land, as they are this day." Deut. 28:25-28 ESV.

As the Lord yearned to gain the Israelites' devotion, the signs and wonders once used to deliver His people would be used for their demise. "All these curses shall come upon you and pursue you and overtake you till you are destroyed, because you did not obey the voice of the Lord your God, to keep his commandments and his statutes that he commanded you. They shall be a sign and a wonder against you and your offspring forever." Deut. 28:45-46 ESV. The people set apart in praise, fame, and honor above all nations would become a horror to all the kingdoms of the earth.

Longing to impart the seriousness of the covenant under which they lived, Moses continued, "Whereas you were as numerous as the stars of the heaven, you shall be left few in number, because you did not obey the voice of the Lord your God. And as the Lord took delight in doing you good and multiplying you, so the Lord will take delight in bringing ruin upon you and destroying you. And you shall be plucked off the land that you are entering to take possession of it. And the Lord will scatter you among all peoples, from one end of the earth to the other, and there you shall serve other gods of wood and stone, which neither you nor your fathers have known. And among these nations you shall find no respite, and there shall be no resting place for the sole of your foot, but the Lord will give you there a trembling heart and failing eyes and a languishing soul." Deut. 28:62-65 ESV.

These words echo through time and provide a haunting picture of the path upon which Israel has traveled. As the people established to be holy unto the Father have strayed from their unique calling, their history portrays the faithfulness of the Almighty both in discipline and blessing. While they may be scattered, a faithful remnant will always remain, standing in the gap and maintaining the promises of old. What an enormous price our Father has placed upon covenant and obedience. For a covenant to exist, it must have first been offered and accepted. With the acceptance, each party voluntarily submits to the terms and conditions outlined within the agreement. While our Father is One of justice, He abounds also with gentility and love, patiently waiting and desiring for us to receive the covenant offered. Never will He force His will upon us. Although offered freely, the covenant carries with it requirements and conditions upon its acceptance. As the nation molded by the hand of the Father accepted the covenant extended, they submitted to the conditions outlined and stepped forth as God's chosen nation. While time traveled forward and the nature of sin swirled, the Israelites transgressed and broke their covenant with the Almighty. Because they had accepted the covenant extended, the consequences for violating the relationship were severe. How the Father must have longed for His people to truly grasp the enormity of their covenant, to walk in full submission and obedience along the path created specifically for their calling. How He longs for the hearts of all to beat in time with His own, remembering and embracing in entirety the covenant and redemption offered.

After wandering forty years, the generation destined to receive the land of promise stepped through the waters of the Jordan under Joshua's guidance. Emerging cleansed and renewed, the nation set apart as holy and treasured walked forward with the empowerment to fulfill a destiny everlasting. Nations trembled and hearts melted as the God of the Israelites entered the land. The people of Jericho sought refuge behind walls erected by earthly hands but destined to be laid in ruin by the very breath of the Israelites. In spite of a miraculous victory, the entirety of Israel did not walk in obedience to the conditions established by the Father, and devoted items were taken against instruction. While these items remained hidden beneath Achan's tent, the Israelites advanced upon the settlement of Ai, anticipating the hand of the Father to again move on their behalf. As fortunes reversed, the Israelites suffered and fled, their hearts of courage melting as water.

As Joshua cried out to the Lord, He responded, "Israel has sinned; they have transgressed my covenant that I commanded them; they have taken some of the devoted things; they have lied and put them among their own belongings. Therefore the people of Israel cannot stand before their enemies. They turn their backs before their enemies, because they have become devoted for destruction. I will be with you no more, unless you destroy the devoted things from among you." Joshua 7: 11-12 ESV.

The violation of the covenant by Achan committed to death thirty-six of the Israelite men as well as Achan's entire family and all that he owned. What an enormous price our Father places upon total obedience. While justice must be served, He is always faithful to provide a way to return. Just as He advised Joshua of the transgression and retribution required, so also He whispers to us our shortcomings and longs for a repentant, obedient heart. As Joshua moved in obedience, the Lord's presence was restored and victory granted over the people of Ai. Following the conquest, the Israelites were this time granted permission to receive the plunder for themselves.[7]

After victory, peace, and land had been granted, the Israelites elected to forfeit a piece of their uniqueness and desired an earthly king. Despite walking with the Father as no other, the Israelites elected to absorb aspects of the nations around, stepping ever nearer to the cliff of disobedience. The path of

---

[7] Joshua Chapters 7-8.

their choosing would be replete with trials yet unseen or fully understood. As the Israelites transitioned from Saul to David to Solomon, they walked intermittently in His ways. After the temple was complete, the Lord appeared to Solomon and restated the conditions of their covenant and the consequences which would flow from transgression.

Reminiscent of the words spoken previously by Moses, the Lord again reminded His people of the importance of obedience. "But if you turn aside and forsake my statutes and my commandments that I have set before you and go and serve other gods and worship them, then I will pluck you up from my land that I have given you and this house that I have consecrated for my name, I will cast out of my sight and I will make it a proverb and a byword among all peoples. And at this house, which was exalted, everyone passing by will be astonished and say, 'Why has the Lord done thus to this land to this house?' Then they will say, 'Because they abandoned the Lord, the God of their fathers who brought them out of the land of Egypt and laid hold on other gods and worshiped them and served them. Therefore he has brought all this disaster on them.'" 2 Chronicles 7:19-22 ESV.

As the nations gazed upon the Israelites, they envisioned clearly the One from whom the true power flowed. In spite of miracles innumerable and feats indescribable, the nation treasured above all failed to fully grasp her relationship with the Father. Shining forth as a light to the nations, the Israelites illuminated the might and devotion of the Almighty, and the fear of the Lord reverberated throughout the land. What the multitudes discerned clearly, the chosen nation failed to truly comprehend. While the world trembled in fear and reverence of the Almighty, the Israelites departed from the One who had crafted them into a nation unique and wrought a deliverance unimaginable.

Following the death of Solomon, the people molded by the Father were divided into the kingdoms of Israel and Judah, as the consequences of disobedience began to carve an indelible path. The tribes of Benjamin and Judah were united under Rehoboam as the nation of Judah, while the remaining ten tribes followed Jeroboam as the kingdom of Israel. Because of Solomon's transgressions, the majority of the tribes were granted to the hand of Jeroboam with the promise of the Lord's protection and provision if they walked in His ways. While the nation of Judah would bear the consequences of disobedience, the affliction would not be everlasting, as the faithful remnant and the Davidic covenant would preserve the promises of old. As His words echoed through the ages, the Lord's protective hand was restored over the land of Judah when they humbly returned to the ways of their fathers. As years passed, battles waged between the kingdoms created to walk as one under the breath of the Almighty.[8]

As the multitudes of Ammon, Moab, and Mount Seir

---

[8] For a thorough history of the reigns of Rehoboam and Jeroboam, see 1 Kings Chapters 11-14 and 2 Chronicles Chapters 10-12.

gathered against Judah, the Lord spoke through a Levite within their midst, "….. Do not be afraid and do not be dismayed at this great horde, for the battle is not yours but God's. You will not need to fight in this battle. Stand firm, hold your position, and see the salvation of the Lord on your behalf, O Judah and Jerusalem. Do not be afraid and do not be dismayed. Tomorrow go out against them, and the Lord will be with you." 2 Chronicles 20:15, 17 ESV.

Within these words, the heart of the Father rings through, as He longs to impart the depth of His devotion and care. While multitudes raged and logic strove to overcome, the battle would not be theirs. The very One from whom all creation flowed, Who breathed life and beauty into all, would fight on their behalf, wielding the sword of destruction against any who dared to approach the nation set apart as His own. The outcome had already been granted, and the victory won. They need only stand, stand in obedience to His call and ways, and the deliverance would come as it had so many times prior. Through the seemingly simple command to stand, the price of protection was revealed. Although outwardly unassuming, the price exacted would be one requiring total, complete obedience and reliance upon the Father. The tribes of Israel and Judah fluctuated between submission and transgression, experiencing riches, honor, and peace in times of faithfulness while enduring trials and hardships as they wandered from their Father. How the Father longs for His people to grasp the essence of His nature, to know within their spirits that He yearns to redeem and deliver, to fight on their behalf. How He longs for us to walk in the victory and might which has already been granted at the cost of His absolute all. Calling us to remember, He desires a creation sustained by His every heartbeat and breath, exhaling the spirit of obedience.

"Take care, lest you forget the covenant of the Lord your God, which he made with you, and make a carved image, the form of anything that the Lord your God has forbidden you. For the Lord your God is a consuming fire, a jealous God. When you father children and children's children, and have grown old in the land, if you act corruptly by making a carved image in the form of anything, and by doing what is evil in the sight of the Lord your God, so as to provoke him to anger, I will call heaven and earth to witness against you today, that you will soon utterly perish from the land that you are going over the Jordan to possess. You will not live long in it, but will be utterly destroyed. And the Lord will scatter you among the peoples, and you will be left few in number among the nations where the Lord will drive you. And there you will serve gods of wood and stone, the work of human hands, that neither see, nor hear, nor eat, nor smell. But from there you will seek the Lord your God and you will find him, if you search after him with all your heart and with all your soul. When you are in tribulation, and all these things come upon you in the latter days, you will return to the Lord your God and obey his voice. For the Lord your

God is a merciful God. He will not leave you or destroy you or forget the covenant with your fathers that he swore to them." Deuteronomy 4:23-31 ESV.

Within this passage, hope springs forth, hope for the nation of Israel to return to her calling and walk in accordance with the ways of the Creator. A glimmer of future shines through, illuminating the promise of God's treasured nation walking in obedience to the God of her fathers and fulfilling the destiny for which she was created. As Christians grafted into His covenant, anticipation and assurance abounds, as His words echo the promise of a covenant never forgotten.

Just as hope resounds, so also resonates the accompanying precaution, "Take care, lest you forget the covenant of the Lord your God." Deuteronomy 4:23 ESV. How He longs for us to remember and truly comprehend all that is enveloped within a covenant. Wrapped within the covenant extended is the expectation of obedience. While the price for forsaking the Father is staggering, He is forever near, sustaining His promises through a faithful remnant and yearning for all to seek Him. When we search with all our heart and soul, when we return in obedience to the Lord, He is faithful always to redeem, to fight on our behalf and wield the mighty hand of judgment against our adversaries. He is merciful, watching eternally and seeking continually for a reason to redeem. While consequences for disobedience must ensue, He will not devote to destruction the entirety of His creation or forget the covenant extended to His people and offered to the nations through the blood of Jesus.

We as Christians must also remember the covenant, understand the implications contained therein, and truly grasp its meaning. In the midst of our total depravity, He stretched out through the body of a carpenter and offered a covenant to His creation, the opportunity to stand with His treasured nation and receive the salvation He so longs to impart. If we would pause and reflect upon the enormity of the covenant extended and truly feel the beat of His heart, we would re-awaken to a love and devotion which knows no end, wrapped inside a gift of unimaginable proportions and the highest cost. While we have tread in accordance with the beating of our own hearts, He has watched, waiting patiently for us to reach the end of ourselves and turn from wayward paths to that which is straight and narrow. Desiring that we would seek Him with every ounce of our beings, He stands with outstretched arms, longing for His creation to repent of their ways and return to the mercy and salvation He longs to deliver. A God of covenants awaits, desiring relationships with His creation, longing for us to feel the beat of His heart and grasp His true nature. As we understand His expression of covenant, we perceive His language of obedience, while we learn to stand faithful and true, illuminating His love to a world in need. Our God of covenants is waiting to be found.

15

A Thread of Heritage
Jewish Wedding Ceremony

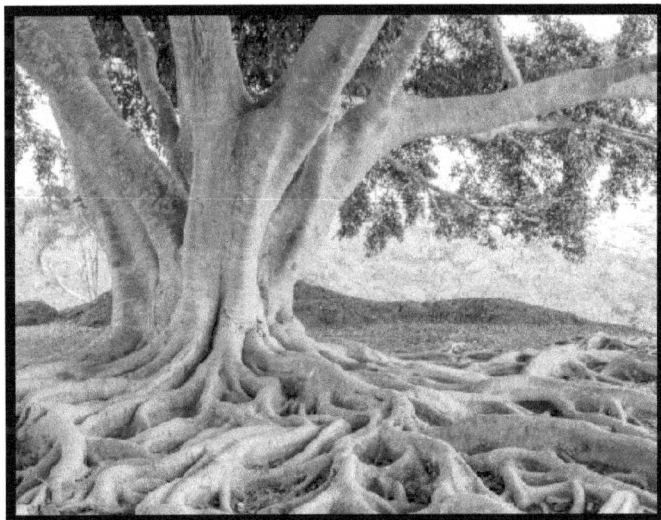

"Then I heard what seemed to be the voice of a great multitude, like the roar of many waters and like the sound of mighty peals of thunder, crying out,

'Hallelujah!

For the Lord our God

the Almighty reigns.

Let us rejoice and exult

and give him the glory,

For the marriage of the Lamb has come,

and his Bride has made herself ready;

It was granted her to clothe herself

With fine linen, bright and pure'

For the fine linen is the righteous deeds of the saints.

And the angel said to me, 'Write this: Blessed are those who are invited to the marriage supper of the Lamb.' And he said to me, 'These are the true words of God.'" Revelation 19: 6-9 ESV.

Within the words of John, mysteries are unveiled and a festival foretold, bringing to culmination the completion of the Father's plan and the victory bought at the greatest of costs. While we as Christians recognize the church as the bride of

Christ, the true beauty and depth of the relationship portrayed often remains concealed within the folds of Jewish heritage. To truly understand the depth of symbolism wrapped within these verses, a glimpse into the Jewish wedding ceremony is invaluable.

"Now the birth of Jesus Christ took place in this way. When his mother Mary had been betrothed to Joseph, before they came together she was found to be with child from the Holy Spirit. And her husband Joseph, being a just man and unwilling to put her to shame, resolved to divorce her quietly." Matthew 1:18-19 ESV.

Within Jewish tradition, the pathway to marriage began with the betrothal ceremony. Beginning as an agreement between families, the covenant relationship of marriage was initiated with the betrothal. With the support of their communities, the new couple gathered with families and friends in joyful celebration of lives now woven inextricably together. As the festivities continued, it was customary for the couple to exchange rings and sign the ketubah, an agreement which established the couple's mutual commitment to each other. Often, the ketubah recounted the price the groom had paid for his bride, just as Jesus has also paid a cost for each of us. From this point forward, the couple was considered to be married in all respects except physically. The betrothal was considered so seriously that it was only severed with a bill of divorce.

According to custom, the groom would thereafter leave to prepare a house in anticipation of his new bride. The time of his return would remain undisclosed even to his bride. Stepping forth into a life previously unknown, the groom worked diligently to establish a home and life for his betrothed, yearning for the day when they might be re-united. Typically, the new dwelling would be established upon land belonging to the groom's father or connected to the father's house. Left for a time with her family, the bride was also is charged with a responsibility, readying herself continually for the unknown return of her beloved. Because the time and date of the groom's return was undetermined, the bride needed to always be ready. With anticipation, the bride prepared, desiring that all be perfect and complete at the time appointed for her groom's re-appearance, ready at a moment's notice to begin a life anew.

So also must we be ready, as the time and date of our Messiah's return remains veiled. Although our Groom no longer treads physically upon the earth, He remains forever near, watching and arranging a place for us, his bride. As the disciples struggled to comprehend that which they could not yet grasp, the Savior reassured. "Let not your hearts be troubled. Believe in God, believe also in me. In my Father's house are many rooms. If it were not so, would I have told you that I go to prepare a place for you? And if I go and prepare a place for you, I will come again and will take you to myself, that where I am you may be also. And you know the way to where I am going." John

14:1-4 ESV.

Suddenly, within the midst of the mundane, a shofar might ring throughout the village, breaking the tranquility of a day and ushering in excitement unbridled. With the departure of the groom, a single man had been selected and granted the privilege of announcing the groom's return for his bride. At the sound of the shofar, daily activity paused momentarily before bursting forth with a flurry of anticipation and hasty preparation for the wedding ceremony. The chuppah was collected, the bride adorned, and the community gathered. Wherever the groom first saw his bride, the chuppah was erected, whether a village market or quiet country path. Comprised of a square cloth supported by four poles, the chuppah provided a canopy under which the couple would be married. Because the date and time of the groom's return was unknown, it was customary for the bride's father to also have wedding clothes for the guests as they hurried in from the fields or daily work.

With the community gathered and the bride and groom under the chuppah, the rabbi conducted the wedding ceremony. Wrapped within this second celebration were traditions replete with symbolism. As outlined in the ketubah, two lives merged into one, woven together through the covenant of marriage. With the breaking of a glass, the couple acknowledged the shattering of an old life and ways which could never be mended. As the bride and groom embarked upon a life anew, the rabbi would bestow seven traditional blessings upon the couple, recounting the goodness of God and representing the completion and perfection wrapped within the marriage covenant. The number of completion was also illustrated as the bride customarily circled her groom seven times. Following the ceremony, the marriage was consummated and the celebratory supper commenced. As the community celebrated the new couple and covenant established, the festival would continue for up to seven days.

If we would pause and linger upon the traditions enveloped within the Jewish wedding ceremony, we would see not only a portrait of Jesus and His church but also the portrayal of covenant. As the thread of time has woven from the days of old, the idea of a covenant has permeated each strand, revealing the beat of the Father's heart and the very reason for our existence. As He glanced upon the creation formed with his very breath, the Lord saw that man was not meant to be alone. Within our very core is woven the innate need for intimacy, a longing for relationship with our Father and with those within our midst. Yearning always to draw ever nearer to His creation, our Father has provided for us the template by which we may prosper and live in the harmony envisioned from the beginning of time. Revealing his heart of love through a steadfast hand, He has provided a history of covenants, illustrating over and over His hand of provision and justice. While we were yet sinners, filthy and drowning within our own self-reliance, He stretched out through the body of Jesus and offered the atonement necessary to restore a relationship shattered by sin. Jesus, the perfection of the Father contained within the body of a man, allowed complete vulnerability to flow to a humanity undeserving and entrapped within their own desires. Selfless, perfect love coursed through the veins of Jesus as He stretched forth upon the cross, providing for all an opportunity unimagined while demonstrating servanthood, leadership, and submission unrivaled and perfect. Watching evermore from above, our Father decided to love when we were not lovely, to stand by when we were unfaithful, to again reach forth with a cost inconceivable to reveal a heart abounding with the most true, genuine love. In stark contrast to the ways of the world, pure love stands as a decision rather than a feeling.

As our Father spoke forth creation, he placed within perfection the embodiment of a covenant, establishing humanity with Adam and Eve. As time has coursed through history, the institution of marriage has served as an example of a covenant, providing a vision of relationships as intended and a greater realization of our bond with the Father. Under the leadership of the Father, marriage stands as the foundation of our society. As we are bound together as husband and wife under the covenant of marriage, so also are we bound to our Creator. With reverence and permanence should our vows shine forth, illuminating the language of the Father and covenant to a world swirling in darkness. Not only should we live in marriage with our spouse in every sense of a covenant, but we as Christians should also live in covenant with our Heavenly Father, preparing always for His return. Within the words of Isaiah 62 we find, "For as a young man marries a young woman, so shall your sons marry you, and as the bridegroom rejoices over the bride, so shall your God rejoice over you." Isaiah 65:5 ESV. What a beautiful illustration of times peering forth over the horizon. As we complete the busyness of our days, do we stand ready to join our bridegroom? Upon His triumphant return at trumpet blast, will He recognize the bride He has longed to embrace? With joy abounding, He waits.

"I will greatly rejoice in the Lord; my soul shall exult in my God, for he has clothed me with the garments of salvation; he has covered me with the robe of righteousness, as a bridegroom decks himself like a priest with a beautiful headdress, and as a bride adorns herself with her jewels." Isaiah 61:10 ESV.

As Isaiah prophesied to a nation divided and rebellious, he relayed the Father's heart of justice and faithfulness. Anointed to bring good news to the poor and liberty to the captives, Isaiah spoke of a time to come, a time when Israel will exult also in her God, standing clothed with garments of salvation and robes of righteousness. The picture of a wedding emerges as our priest and bridegroom returns to a bride adorned in finery.

"And again Jesus spoke to them in parables, saying, 'The kingdom of heaven may be compared to a king who gave a wedding feast for his son, and sent his servants to call those who were invited to the wedding feast, but they would not come. Again he sent other servants, saying, 'Tell those who are invited, "See, I have prepared my dinner, my oxen and my fat calves have been slaughtered, and everything is ready. Come to the wedding feast."' But they paid no attention and went off, one to his farm, another to his business, while the rest seized his servants, treated them shamefully, and killed them. The king was angry, and he sent his troops and destroyed those murderers and burned their city. Then he said to his servants, 'The wedding feast is ready, but those invited were not worthy. Go therefore to the main roads and invite to the wedding feast as many as you find.' And those servants went out into the roads and gathered all whom they found, both bad and good. So the wedding hall was filled with guests.

But when the king came in to look at the guests, he saw there a man who had no wedding garment. And he said to him, 'Friend, how did you get in here without a wedding garment?' And he was speechless. Then the king said to the attendants, 'Bind him hand and foot and cast him into the outer darkness. In that place there will be weeping and gnashing of teeth.' For many are called, but few are chosen." Matthew 22:1-14 ESV.

Centuries later, Jesus spoke to His followers, relating truths within the context of traditions which they could understand. Wrapped within the marriage ceremony and covenant were precepts resounding through the ages and the beat of a Father's heart. As Jesus addressed the multitudes through parables, He longed for them to grasp the enormity of things to come, to stand in eager readiness for the garment of salvation and light, illuminating the One Who gave His all. Through His ultimate sacrifice, we are able to emerge as new creatures, casting off darkness and flesh and walking in the reconciliation and victory wrought from days of old. He longs for us to halt the busyness of our days, to truly inhale His nature, and to live in full submission and covenant. At the triumphant blast of the trumpet, let us be found as a bride adorned with the finery of righteousness and salvation bought at an extraordinary cost. Let us stand in full submission, praise, and covenant to the bridegroom who longs to collect his bride.

"Then the kingdom of heaven will be like ten virgins who took their lamps and went to meet the bridegroom. Five of them were foolish, and five were wise. For when the foolish took their lamps, they took no oil with them, but the wise took flasks of oil with their lamps. As the bridegroom was delayed, they all became drowsy and slept. But at midnight there was a cry, 'Here is the bridegroom! Come out to meet him.' Then all those virgins rose and trimmed their lamps. And the foolish said to the wise, 'Give us some of your oil, for our lamps are going out.' But the wise answered, saying, 'Since there will not be enough for us and for you, go rather to the dealers and buy for yourselves.' And while they were going to buy, the bridegroom came, and those who were ready went in with him to the marriage feast, and the door was shut. Afterward the other virgins came also, saying, 'Lord, Lord, open to us.' But he answered 'Truly, I say to you, I do not know you.' Watch therefore, for you know neither the day nor the hour." Matthew 25:1-13 ESV.

As we glean the truths wrapped within the traditional Jewish wedding, let us prepare for our Groom's return and the glorious marriage feast to come. Let not the fullness of our days and self-imposed agendas conceal the vision of our Groom. Let us wait in anticipation, clothed in wedding garments fine, bright, and pure - garments purchased at a price unthinkable by a Father breathing reconciliation. Let us labor dressed in splendid righteousness, shining forth the heart of our Father to a world dark and dreary. Let us exult in the One Who gave His all, yearning, readying, and watching for the return of our Groom. Let us not be caught off guard.

Tapestry Of Roots: Threads Woven By The Master

16

Biblical History of Covenant
The New Covenant

"And when the hour came, he reclined at table, and the apostles with him. And he said to them, 'I have earnestly desired to eat this Passover with you before I suffer. For I tell you I will not eat it until it is fulfilled in the kingdom of God.' And he took a cup, and when he had given thanks he said, 'Take this, and divide it among yourselves. For I tell you that from now on I will not drink of the fruit of the vine until the kingdom of God comes.' And he took bread, and when he had given thanks, he broke it and gave it to them, saying, 'This is my body, which is given for you. Do this in remembrance of me.' And likewise the cup after they had eaten, saying, 'This cup that is poured out for you is the new covenant in my blood.'" Luke 22:14-20 ESV.

As Jesus and the apostles gathered in celebration of the Passover, the heart of the Father breathed words replete with meaning yet spoken to those incapable of fully understanding. As bread was broken and cups passed, a new covenant was offered, the long awaited promise foretold by the prophets and anticipated for centuries. A plan woven from the beginning of time was drawing to fulfillment in the most unlikely of ways, allowing hope and reconciliation to bloom amidst atrocities inconceivable and fear unimaginable. As the heart of the Father laid bare, His only Son provided the atonement for our transgressions and rose again, defeating forevermore the clutch of sin and death. While others have been resurrected, only Jesus has risen Himself, overcoming for eternity all which entraps and offering the opportunity to walk in the victory envisioned through the ages. The new covenant flowing forth from the veins of our beloved Savior is known as a kingly grant, an offer extended to those unworthy with the condition only of belief. Gathered with His disciples on the night which would resound through history, the Father again stretched forth to His beloved creation, offering the long awaited new covenant. In the moments of silence, Jesus spoke, filling the chamber with hope rising through suffering; hope shining forth through a new covenant and the coming kingdom of God. As time travels forward, our beloved Savior waits for us, while days journey to fulfillment and His kingdom approaches. Although crowds gathered, leaders schemed, and wickedness swirled, the thread of the Master wove a tapestry of salvation, turning what was contrived by the leaders as destruction into the blessing prophesied from days of old. Through His resurrection, the victory was granted. While we as Christians understand our reconciliation to the Father through the New Covenant, we must return to the ancient promises to truly comprehend the depth wrapped within the offer. Although often overlooked, the origins of the New Covenant are traced back to the prophets, centuries before the events recorded in the gospels.

Returning as far back as Genesis, we find "Now the Lord said to Abram, 'Go from your country and your kindred and your father's house to the land that I will show you. And I will make of you a great nation, and I will bless you and make your name great, so that you will be a blessing. I will bless those who bless you, and him who dishonors you I will curse, and in you all the families of the earth shall be blessed.'" Genesis 12:1-3 ESV.

Within the beginning words of Scripture, a glimpse of the plan is revealed and a hint disclosed. While time traversed through the ages, the thread continued unbroken, intricately weaving a design of miraculous proportion destined to bring blessing to the nations. This blessing foretells a purpose still impossible to conceive, a plan bought at the highest of costs. The hint of a covenant shines through, a covenant which would include all nations, bringing blessing and reconciliation desired from the breath of creation. Though it remained yet unspoken, the new covenant would flow forth allowing all nations to be grafted into that chosen by the Father.

As Moses spoke to a nation newly crafted and delivered, he provided another glimpse of a time far in the distance, a time not yet conceived. Within the words of the Sh'ma, we find, "Hear, O Israel: the Lord our God, the Lord is one. You shall love the Lord your God with all your heart and with all your soul and with all your might. And these words that I command you this day shall be upon your heart." Deuteronomy 6: 4-6 ESV. Foretelling a time when His instructions would be within our beings, the Father spoke through Moses, bringing hope of a day when His words would be inscribed upon our very hearts empowering us to walk in obedience. A new covenant would one day issue forth ushering the redemption and fellowship orchestrated since creation's breath.

As the thread continued, a greater piece of the tapestry unrolled, revealing another aspect of the covenant designed to reach the nations. Through the Father's words spoken by Nathan the prophet, we learn of the sovereignty of the line of David and a Messiah promised to bring redemption to the world. " ... Moreover, the Lord declares to you that the Lord will make you a house. When your days are fulfilled and you lie down with your fathers, I will raise up your offspring after you, who shall come from your body, and I will establish his kingdom. He shall build a house for my name, and I will establish the throne of his kingdom forever. I will be to him a father, and he shall be to me a son. When he commits iniquity, I will discipline him with the rod of men, with the stripes of the sons of men, but my steadfast love will not depart from him, as I took it from Saul, whom I put away from before you. And your house and your kingdom shall be made sure forever before me. Your throne shall be established forever." 2 Samuel 7: 11-16 ESV.

A scene was illustrated, depicting promises of old embellished with thrones, kingship, and eternity. As Nathan's words filled the air surrounding, a dual prophecy was unveiled, one relating specifically to Solomon and a further meaning finding its fulfillment centuries later through Jesus. Breathing encouragement to David, the Almighty promised a father and kingdom for David's earthly son Solomon. Pledging to remain forever near, the Father breathed words of hope to the one who walked after His own heart, vowing to be to Solomon as a father, guiding and disciplining as necessary, yet abounding with love which would know no end. While Solomon built an earthly house for the Almighty, the true kingdom and Cornerstone were yet to come. Wrapped also within the words of Nathan were promises extending forevermore, introducing a kingship which would last for eternity. Stretching far beyond the comprehension of those to whom it was spoken, this kingship would follow a path unexpected and offer a victory gained through means unfathomed. The breath of the Father continued to weave a remarkable tapestry of redemption as He established a kingdom without end.

Following the thread of time, we see a nation crafted meticulously by the hand of the Father, a people of twelve tribes designed to walk as one. Embarking upon a path of her own choosing and in likeness with the surrounding nations, those set apart as unique walked under the guidance of earthly kings, experiencing the repercussions forewarned. Stumbling under the fallibility of earthly rulers, the nation of Israel failed to see her destiny and the enormity of the covenant under which she breathed. As trials ensued and the Father grieved, the nation crafted as one divided in two. Even so, in the midst of her division, the heart of the Father rang through, longing for His people to truly know the magnitude of her call and His heartbeat of faithfulness. While in the midst of disobedience, He stretched forth with words of judgment but also words of hope, yearning that they feel His breath and walk in the love He so desired. As Israel continued along the divided path, prophets abounded, beseeching repentance and a renewed recognition of the One to Whom they belonged. Although they had walked with the Father as none before, the true beat of His heart remained just beyond understanding's grasp. For true reconciliation, a new covenant would be required, a covenant which would bring empowerment to obey, one in which He would reside within their actual beings and which would inscribe His laws upon their very hearts. Promises were still to come and fulfillment yet to be granted. A new covenant remained veiled, one beyond comprehension which would allow the cycle of sin to be forever broken and forgiveness granted forevermore.

"Incline your ear, and come to me;

hear, that your soul may live;

and I will make with you an everlasting covenant,

my steadfast, sure love for David.

Behold, I made him a witness to the peoples,

a leader and commander for the peoples.

Behold, you shall call a nation that you do not know,

and a nation that did not know you shall run to you,

because of the Lord your God, and of the Holy One of Israel,

for he has glorified you." Isaiah 55: 3-5 ESV.

Through the words of Isaiah, the Father pleaded, longing for His nation to walk in the destiny for which she was created. Chosen and molded by the Almighty's hands, Israel received the Father's breath, instilling a unique calling and a mission designed to stretch to the ends of the earth. Pleading to those struggling within a nation divided, Isaiah provided another glimpse of the tapestry of redemption and the fulfillment of promises of old. Israel, destined to call a nation that did not know the Lord, was designed to illuminate the Holy One of Israel, illustrating in perfection His nature, covenants, and heart that beats for His own. As Israel walks in her destiny and the thread travels forward, the nations will run to the Father, to the God revealed through Israel. How far we have strayed. How the heart of the Father must grieve when we as Christians do not run to those from Whom the covenant flows and through Whom the greatest of all gifts was offered.

"I was ready to be sought by those who did not ask for me;

I was ready to be found by those who did not seek me.

I said, 'Here I am, here I am,' to a nation that was not called

by my name." Isaiah 65: 1 ESV.

"Here I am." With the utterance of this impassioned plea,

the heart of our Lord is laid bare as He cries out through the words of Isaiah, longing, yearning, entreating, so that He might in turn bring upon the nations the blessings He so longs to give. The design for worldwide redemption was further unveiled, although the rebellious heart of man continued to beat in accordance with his own desires. A time unimaginable rested just below the horizon, a time when His covenant would be extended to all, Jew and Gentile alike. A promised Messiah was coming, with an unlikely plan of victory, ushering in the fulfillment of words breathed centuries prior and bringing reconciliation to all. For this, a new covenant would be necessary, not because the old was flawed, but because the people were fallible and incapable of fulfilling the requirements upon their own merit. With a heart abounding in love, the Father watched as the nation crafted by His very hands struggled. As sin swirled and rebellion mounted, a cycle emerged, one of repeated discretion, correction, repentance, and restoration. The sinful nature of man would necessitate a change within his very heart, a change which would bring the full restoration envisioned through the ages. While the Law remains infallible, the heart of man beats with iniquity. Rather than any imperfection discovered, the need for a new covenant rested within the heart of the man to whom it was granted. The Law serves as stipulations and conditions to the agreement between the Father and Israel, but it is not of itself the covenant. Instead, the covenant resides in the relationship designed and offered by the Almighty's hand.

Throughout the time of division and exile, the Father breathed hope into a people downtrodden and rebellious, stretching forth through the prophets to introduce the new covenant. Although often overlooked, the true origins of the new covenant rest within the words of the Old Testament, and its promises were extended to the nation of Israel.

"Behold, the days are coming, declares the Lord, when I will make a new covenant with the house of Israel and the house of Judah, not like the covenant that I made with their fathers on the day when I took them by the hand to bring them out of the land of Egypt, my covenant that they broke, though I was their husband, declares the Lord. But this is the covenant that I will make with the house of Israel after those days, declares the Lord: I will put my law within them, and I will write it on their hearts. And I will be their God, and they shall be my people. And no longer shall each one teach his neighbor and each his brother, saying 'Know the Lord,' for they shall all know me, from the least of them to the greatest, declares the Lord. For I will forgive their iniquity, and I will remember their sin no more." Jeremiah 31:31-34 ESV.

Yearning to be their God, the Lord spoke to His treasured nation, imparting hope and a glimpse of a time yet to arrive. While the mighty forces of Babylon loomed and destruction threatened, the Father breathed anticipation into hearts heavy. Stretching forth with love unfathomable, the Father foretold the new covenant to come, one which built upon promises of old and inscribed His law within their very beings. Rather than existing outside as a standard to attain, the Law would be a part of them, beating in tune with the Father and providing the ability to attain what the written Law could not. They would be wholly His, treading forth in belief and obedience, forgiven and redeemed. Hearts of stone would be replaced with circumcised, pliable hearts receptive to His leading and submitted to the One who provides their all.

"Behold, I will gather them from all the countries to which I drove them in my anger and my wrath and in great indignation. I will bring them back to this place, and I will make them dwell in safety. And they shall be my people, and I will be their God. I will give them one heart and one way, that they may fear me forever, for their own good and the good of their children after them. I will make them an everlasting covenant, that I will not turn away from doing good to them. And I will put the fear of me in their hearts, that they may not turn from me. I will rejoice in doing them good, and I will plant them in this land in faithfulness, with all my heart and all my soul." Jeremiah 32: 37-41 ESV.

"Behold, the days are coming, declares the Lord, when I will fulfill the promise I made to the house of Israel and the house of Judah. In those days and at that time I will cause a righteous Branch to spring up for David, and he shall execute justice and righteousness in the land. In those days Judah will be saved, and Jerusalem will dwell securely. And this is the name by which it will be called: 'The Lord is our righteousness.'

For thus says the Lord: 'David shall never lack a man to sit on the throne of the house of Israel, and the Levitical priests shall never lack a man in my presence to offer burnt offerings, to burn grain offerings, and to make sacrifices forever.'

The word of the Lord came to Jeremiah: 'Thus says the Lord: If you can break my covenant with the day and my covenant with the night, so that day and night will not come at their appointed time, then also my covenant with David my servant may be broken, so that he shall not have a son to reign on his throne, and my covenant with the Levitical priests my ministers. As the host of heaven cannot be numbered and the sands of the sea cannot be measured, so I will multiply the offspring of David my servant, and the Levitical priests who minister to me.'

The word of the Lord came to Jeremiah: 'Have you not observed these people saying, 'The Lord has rejected the two clans that he chose?' Thus says the Lord, if I have not established my covenant with day and night and the fixed order of heaven and earth, then I will reject the offspring of Jacob and David my servant and will not choose one of his offspring to rule over the offspring of Abraham, Isaac, and Jacob. For I will restore their fortunes and will have mercy on them.'" Jeremiah 33:14-26 ESV.

As Jeremiah continued, rays of hope illuminated the horizon, foretelling a Messianic age to come and confirming that the Father's nation would not be rejected. Just as we cannot order the passage of the day, so can we not alter the destiny of those crafted by the very hand of God. As the promises of old ring true, a day will burst upon the horizon when Israel will be saved, when the land of Israel will dwell in safety, and a Jewish Messiah will reign forevermore. Speaking to a nation divided, Jeremiah foretold unification, a time with one heart and one way uniform in obedience to the Almighty. The cycle of sin will one day be destroyed.

"I will take you from the nations and gather you from all the countries and bring you into your own land. I will sprinkle clean water on you, and you shall be clean from all your uncleanness, and from all your idols I will cleanse you. And I will give you a new heart, and a new spirit I will put within you. And I will remove the heart of stone from your flesh and give you a heart of flesh. And I will put my Spirit within you, and cause you to walk in my statutes and be careful to obey my rules. You shall dwell in the land that I gave to your fathers, and you shall be my people, and I will be your God." Ezekiel 36: 24-28 ESV.

Addressing a nation divided, Ezekiel spoke from exile, foretelling a time of spiritual and national renewal. While the people crafted as one breathed divided, hope sprung forth with promises of unity, cleansing, a new heart, and land. Wrapped within these words we find the fulfillment of the new covenant and the Messianic age to come. Through the death and resurrection of Jesus, we are cleansed from our iniquities and empowered with the very presence of God within us as the Holy Spirit. Working within us continually to transform and circumcise our hearts of stone, the Father continues to mold and craft His people, longing for us to fully realize the depth of His devotion and intricacy of His plan. While the gift of the Holy Spirit brings empowerment to obey, we struggle continually with the clutch of sin upon our beings. A day is coming, however, when we will know the Father as never before, when His laws will be inscribed upon our hearts in entirety, and when the struggle will succumb fully to the victory attained through His resurrection. There will one day be a universal revelation of our Father, and His people will truly know Him within the core of their beings. Our hearts will be fully flesh, beating with His and pulsing with obedience, changed and completed through the resurrection of Jesus. The fulfillment of the new covenant will bring the redemption designed from the breath of creation, hearts of love reflected through obedience, and the full restoration of relationships with our Father for which all were created.

"... Behold I am about to take the stick of Joseph (that is in the hand of Ephraim) and the tribes of Israel associated with him. And I will join with it the stick of Judah, and make them one stick, that they may be one in my hand. When the sticks on which you write are in your hands before their eyes, then say to them, Thus says the Lord God: Behold, I will take the people of Israel from the nations among which they have gone, and will gather them from all around, and bring them to their own land. And I will make them one nation in the land, on the mountains of Israel. And one king shall be king over them all, and they shall be no longer two nations, and no longer divided into two kingdoms." Ezekiel 37: 19-22 ESV.

Although often overlooked, restoration of the land of Israel is enveloped within the new covenant. As time weaves through history, a tapestry is created as one, reconciling the Jewish people, the land of Israel, and eventually Jew and Gentile. How the Father must yearn for that day! While foretelling events not yet understood, the prophets spoke to the nation divided yet crafted to be a light to the world. One day this new covenant would be extended also to the Gentile, uniting believers in Jesus while retaining values distinctive to their respective callings.

As foretold through the words of Jeremiah and Ezekiel, the Lord began to gather His people from the surrounding nations, restoring as one the nation split from the time of Rehoboam and Jeroboam. Lead by Zerubbabel during the reign of King Cyrus, Ezra in the days of Artaxerxes, and finally by Nehemiah, the Father's people returned to the land of Israel as the period of exile and judgment found completion. Sweeping through the nations, the Father searched and called forth His faithful remnant from each of the twelve tribes, designed and selected for such a time.

"And they stood up in their place and read from the Book of the Law of the Lord their God for a quarter of the day; for another quarter of it they made confession and worshiped the Lord their God." Nehemiah 9:3 ESV.

"Because of all this we make a firm covenant in writing; on the sealed document are the names of our princes, our Levites, and our priests." Nehemiah 9:38 ESV.

With hearts tender, the remnant gathered in fasting and prayer, confessing their iniquities and longing for reconciliation. Recounting their creation, deliverance, and sustenance as a nation, they acknowledged their wayward journey and the unmerited favor of the Father. After enduring hardships innumerable, the Israelites were humbled, softened, and ready to walk submitted to the One Who granted each breath. They remembered. Bowing in repentance, they renewed the covenant originally extended to their forefathers and anticipated the arrival of the new covenant foretold by the prophets. Standing on promises resounding through the ages, the remnant returned to their land with renewed hope, realization, and a desire to walk in the destiny for which they were created. They inhaled and savored the breath of their covenant, longing for and awaiting the promised Messiah. As spiritual renewal poured forth, two sticks reunited as one and flourished once again in the land granted by the Almighty. It would be to this remnant of all twelve tribes that the Messiah would indeed come. The historical books of the Old Testament conclude with the renewed covenant of Nehemiah and a people walking forth in their destiny, shining as a light to the nations and awaiting the promised Messiah.

Before traveling fully into the New Testament, let us examine the better promises wrapped within the new covenant foretold by the prophets. As the Father watched from days of old, He beheld a creation caught within the clutch of sin and engaged in a perpetual struggle to achieve that which He desired, a creation who had failed to grasp the heart intent residing beneath the Law. With the fateful decision in the Garden of Eden, iniquity poured forth, forever encircling and binding the heart of man. As wickedness crept, the Father provided additional laws, desiring that His creation would grasp their inability to fulfill His requirements, their ultimate need for redemption, and the true intent of His heart. All knowing and all powerful, He watched and waited, continually weaving the thread of salvation conceived with creation's breath. Total, complete Perfection gazed upon His creation, yearning to reside within their very beings and willing to pay the ultimate cost required. Ours is a Lord of perfection inconceivable, surety unchanging, and steadfast, boundless love and devotion. The shortcoming in the system rested within the heart of man, not within the law of the Father.

The promises of the new covenant hinge upon the land of Israel and the Father's change within the hearts of His creation. Rather than absolving the laws of the old covenant, the new covenant provides the empowerment to walk as He would desire through the gift of the Holy Spirit. This change sets the new covenant apart from the Mosaic, inscribing His laws upon our hearts and imparting His Spirit to enable obedience. The laws, however, remain the same, as the perfect law of the Father does not change. Expanding upon promises of old, the Father again stretched forth to a nation divided and breathed hope and re-unification through the offer of a new covenant to come. Speaking to the Jewish nation, the Almighty promised a time when they would be empowered by Him to walk in His statutes and obey His ordinances, a time when the nation of Israel would dwell in her own land in safety and security, and a time when forgiveness would be granted as never before. One day, Israel will recognize herself as the Father's, and He will be her God. The nation molded by the Almighty's hand will walk forth in full submission, obedience, and anointing as they usher in the greatest harvest of all time. While the offer of the new covenant was extended prior to the death and resurrection of Christ, it has not yet reached its fulfillment. A time glistens just beyond the horizon when the Law will be fully inscribed upon the hearts of believers, and they will know the Lord as never before. While the resurrection of Jesus allowed the gift of the Holy Spirit and the empowerment to obey, a time is yet to come when we will no longer struggle with our flesh, when the true victory will be realized and the clutch of sin destroyed.

As we leave the pages of the Old Testament, we see the Father's principle of the remnant, gathered as one in the days of Nehemiah and standing upon words breathed through the prophets. Enduring as the faithful few of the twelve tribes, the remnant gathered, interceded, and maintained the promises of old while the majority struggled. They waited, year after year and century upon century, in faithful obedience and intercession for the many, always longing and hoping for the fulfillment of promise. With hearts beating in time to the Father's unchanging devotion, they abided in faith unshakeable. Through centuries of silence, the remnant interceded, waiting, believing, and longing for the promises uttered years prior. Finally, after four hundred years of silence, the Lord stretched forth through the angel Gabriel and breathed renewed hope into His people, bringing to realization the promises foretold and strengthening the hearts sustained by His breath.

"Now when he was serving as priest before God when his division was on duty, according to the custom of the priesthood, he was chosen by lot to enter the temple of the Lord and burn incense. And the whole multitude of the people were praying outside at the hour of incense. And there appeared to him an angel of the Lord standing on the right side of the altar of incense. And Zechariah was troubled when he saw him, and fear fell upon him. But the angel said to him, 'Do not be afraid, Zechariah, for your prayer has been heard, and your wife Elizabeth will bear you a son, and you shall call his name John. And you will have joy and gladness, and many will rejoice at his birth, for he will be great before the Lord. And he must not drink wine or strong drink and he will be filled with the Holy Spirit, even from his mother's womb. And he will turn many of the children of Israel to the Lord their God, and he will go before him in the spirit and power of Elijah, to turn the hearts of the fathers to the children, and the disobedient to the wisdom of the just, to make ready for the Lord a people prepared.'" Luke 1:8-17 ESV.

As the Lord's words flowed through Gabriel, another portrait within the tapestry was unveiled. After centuries of silence, the words of the Father burst forth with clarity and promise, announcing one who would prepare the way for the promised Messiah. As Zechariah served within the temple and the multiples prayed outside, He appeared through Gabriel in an amazing way. Throughout four hundred years, the prayers had mounted, and the faithful had waited. Bursting forth upon the land would be a time of spiritual rebirth, miracles, signs, and wonders. The voice of John would ring through the wilderness, proclaiming a baptism of repentance and forgiveness in preparation for the Son's arrival. The promised Messiah would soon appear, ushering in the will of His Father and bringing restoration and victory in the most unexpected of ways.

"And in the same region there were shepherds out in the field, keeping watch over their flock by night. And an angel of the Lord appeared to them, and the glory of the Lord shone around them, and they were filled with fear. And the angel said to them, 'Fear not, for behold, I bring you good news of great joy that will be for all the people For unto you is born this day in the city of David, a Savior, who is Christ the Lord.'" Luke 2:8-11 ESV.

As the shepherds stood aghast, a miraculous presence appeared, declaring words echoed through history and announcing the long awaited Messiah. With glory illuminating the night sky, the Father stretched forth and revealed further His plan of redemption designed for all. In the small town of Bethlehem, a mighty miracle had taken place, as the very presence of God inhaled the earth's air and breathed in human flesh. Issuing forth from the city of David would be the heart of the Father longing to bring reconciliation to His people, to bind up the broken hearted, and to restore relationships severed by sin. As the Word dwelt among humanity, He longed to be within their very beings, beating within hearts submitted and providing the empowerment to obey. How He must have yearned for all to truly grasp the nature of the Law rather than the mere words. With a mission of immeasurable importance destined to change the entirety of creation, Jesus walked and breathed among the people teaching, loving, and sharing the Father's heart. Through suffering unimaginable and submission unparalleled, He willingly provided the atonement necessary so that all might live. Rising three days later, He was declared the Son of God in power and might, ushering in victory unfathomable and offered freely to those who believed. As foretold by Ezekiel and Jeremiah and maintained since the days of Nehemiah, a new covenant would be offered through the blood of Jesus, a covenant familiar and resounding with truths of old, yet new in depth and complexity. Extended first to the Jew, this new covenant would flow forth also the Gentile, ushering in the blessings to the nations foretold in the Father's original covenant with Abraham.

"Then he said to them, 'These are my words that I spoke to you while I was still with you, that everything written about me in the Law of Moses and the Prophets and the Psalms must be fulfilled.' Then he opened their minds to understand the Scriptures, and said to them, 'Thus it is written, that the Christ should suffer and on the third day rise from the dead, and that repentance and forgiveness of sins should be proclaimed in his name to all nations, beginning from Jerusalem. You are witnesses of these things. And behold, I am sending the promise of my Father upon you. But stay in the city until you are clothed with power from on high.'" Luke 24: 44-49 ESV.

While the disciples gathered in the days following the crucifixion, fear coursed through emotions raw as they struggled to live without their beloved leader. Not fully understanding the depth and repercussions of the preceding hours, they longed to grasp the meaning enveloped within the events unfolded. The One upon Whom rested the hope of Israel's redemption would no longer walk upon the earth, and they wrestled to reconcile recent happenings with promises foretold. Just as His ways and timing are not our own, the Messiah would indeed bring the redemption of Israel, ushering in victory and redemption destined to flow to the nations in the most unlikely of ways. While the long awaited covenant had been extended, its magnitude remained shrouded within tears and sorrow. As the resurrected Christ stood within their midst, their minds were opened and comprehension granted to grasp more deeply the promises and events recounted through the ages. As the veil was withdrawn, the sign of the new covenant was remembered, the gift of the Holy Spirit dwelling within their very beings. Yearning to reside within our core, the Holy Spirit would provide the empowerment to live according to His desires and to walk in the fellowship with our Father envisioned with creation's breath. As the disciples stood in awe and newfound joy and understanding, they were cautioned to remain in the city until the promise was bestowed.

"And it shall come to pass afterward that I will pour out my Spirit on all flesh; your sons and your daughters shall prophesy, your old men shall dream dreams, and our young men shall see visions. Even on the male and female servants in those days I will pour out my Spirit. And I will show wonders in the heavens and on the earth, blood and fire and columns of smoke. The sun shall be turned to darkness, and the moon to blood, before the great and awesome day of the Lord comes. And it shall come to pass that everyone who calls on the name of the Lord shall be saved....." Joel 2: 28-32 ESV.

Centuries prior, the words of Joel echoed through Jerusalem, providing a glimpse of days to come, a time when His Spirit would pour forth with signs and wonders and when salvation would be granted to those calling upon His name. Wrapped within these words is the promise flowing forth through Abraham to the nations, the sign of the new covenant, and hope in our Messiah's return. As the Lord spoke through Joel, the thread of redemption intertwined the desires of His heart, unveiling further His original covenant with Abraham through the promises of salvation and His Spirit to guide forevermore. As the disciples' shrouds of grief unfurled, the words of the prophets and the intricacies of the Father's plan must have resounded through their spirits and created an anticipation indescribable.

Stepping forward into a future unknown, the apostles were despised by many leaders of their faith and commanded not to teach the Messiah's resurrection. While evil threatened to suppress the victory attained, the apostles shone forth, unable to deny that which had been revealed and placed upon their hearts. The Father was drawing ever closer, yearning for His truth to resound through the nations. As Jesus walked the earth following the resurrection, He longed to impart the victory attained and mysteries to be unveiled in the future, a time when the new covenant would be fully realized and when all could know Him within their core, a time when the Comforter would dwell permanently within the bodies of all believers. While the Holy Spirit was previously granted for specific times and purposes, the new covenant promised another gift inconceivable, the very presence of the Father always within man's spirit comforting, teaching, and empowering.

"When the day of Pentecost arrived, they were all together in one place. And suddenly there came from heaven a sound like a mighty rushing wind, and it filled the entire house where they were sitting. And divided tongues as of fire appeared to them and rested on each one of them. And they were all filled with the Holy Spirit and began to speak in other tongues as the Spirit gave them utterance.

Now there were dwelling in Jerusalem Jews, devout men from every nation under heaven. And at this sound the multitude came together, and they were bewildered because each one was hearing them speak in his own language. And they were amazed and astonished, saying, 'Are not all these who are speaking Galileans and how is it that we hear each of us in his own native language? Parthians and Medes and Elamites and residents of Mesopotamia, Judea and Cappadocia, Pontus and Asia, Phrygia and Pamphylia, Egypt and the parts of Libya belonging to Cyrene, and visitors from Rome, both Jews and proselytes, Cretans and Arabians – we hear them telling in our own tongues the mighty works of God.'" Acts 2: 1-11 ESV.

As the apostles gathered for the annual celebration of Shavuot, or Pentecost, the Father's design was further revealed. Ten days had passed since the ascension of their beloved leader, and they waited in eager anticipation of the promised gift, wondering each day if the appointed time had come and longing to grasp the full meaning of the Savior's words. As the Savior departed, He lifted His hands and blessed the disciples. "While he blessed them, he parted from them and was carried up into heaven. And they worshiped him and returned to Jerusalem with great joy, and were continually in the temple blessing God." Luke 24: 51-53 ESV. Following Christ's ascension, the apostles tread as He had walked, relishing His memory and abiding continually within the temple. Cherishing the words spoken through the very flesh of God, they yearned to remain always in His presence, allowing His memory to comfort and assure of days and promises yet to come. Within the courts and surrounded by the walls of the temple, the disciples likely felt closest to their beloved leader, as memories of His words echoed among the columns.

With breath, the Father spoke into existence creation and life into the nostrils of Adam. With the breath of a mighty wind and tongues of fire, He bestowed upon the apostles the long awaited gift of His Spirit and the sign of the new covenant. Not content to merely dwell within our midst or during specified times, He yearned to reside within our very spirits, enabling all to walk in the victory granted and already complete. Granted to all believers would be the permanent indwelling of God Himself, ever present to guide, interpret, and empower. Yearning to renew hearts, to bind the brokenhearted, to lose all that binds, He patiently waits within the hearts of all who believe, longing for His children to walk in the fullness of His power and victory. Within the hearts of all believers lies power inconceivable, victory unsurpassed, and a mission begging to illuminate the Father's love to the nations. While tongues of fire hovered, the words of the Father rang through, extolling His mighty works and boundless love. As the rushing wind flowed forth, His presence filled the apostles, revealing further His plan and fulfilling promises of old.

A look at Acts 2 through the lens of Jewish heritage allows us to grasp more fully the heart of the Almighty and comprehend in greater clarity the events unfolding. As the apostles gathered for the annual festival of Shavuot, or Pentecost, they were joined by Jews and proselytes from the surrounding nations who had journeyed to Jerusalem as directed. Being one of the three festivals which required travel to Jerusalem, the feast of Shavuot brought together Jews scattered throughout the land, assembled as one in obedience, honor, and worship of the One who crafted their very existence. Around the temple courts was an upper perimeter known as Solomon's Colonnade, which contained various rooms used often for study and worship among those with similar interests and trades. This upper area would have allowed the speaker to address those within the immediate area as well as multitudes gathered in the courtyards below. Throughout Christ's ministry, He and the disciples were found frequently within the rooms of the Colonnade, as crowds eagerly awaited each word spoken by the Master. Following in the steps of their beloved leader, Peter and the apostles would have likely gathered within the area of Solomon's Colonnade to celebrate the commanded festival of Shavuot. As a rushing wind permeated the area and the apostles spoke in tongues they had previously not known, the Jewish multitudes gathered in wonder and amazement, hearing the words of the Father in their own language. Assembling within the Colonnade afforded the room necessary for the masses to gather within the Temple perimeter and below as the Holy Spirit flowed forth among the walls and columns to fill the hearts of those who believed.

"And Peter said to them, 'Repent and be baptized every one of you in the name of Jesus Christ for the forgiveness of your sins, and you will receive the gift of the Holy Spirit. For the promise is for you and for your children and for all who are far off, everyone whom the Lord our God calls to himself.'" Acts 2: 38-39 ESV.

Resounding through the words of Peter is the very heart of the Father, longing for all to return, repent, and receive the promise offered and attained at a cost unimaginable. As the

Jews and proselytes (those who had fully converted to Judaism) gathered for the commanded feast of Shavuot, the Father's presence filled the Temple, and the Holy Spirit poured forth into the hearts of those who believed. Although extended only to the Jews at this time, the Father's plan would soon pour forth to the nations, delivering redemption and restoration to all who believed. As the Spirit flowed with might and power through Solomon's Colonnade and the courtyards below, about three thousand were called to repentance and receipt of the gift treasured above all. Gathered for such a time and place were Jews of surrounding nations, brought together through a feast ordained centuries prior yet meticulously orchestrated to provide the gift of His Holy Spirit to thousands. With this, the foundation was established and a new depth added to the relationship He so desired. Rather than stepping forth with a new religion, these infant believers walked forward in their heritage, remembering the promises of old and maintaining the practices established by the Almighty.

"And they devoted themselves to the apostles teaching and the fellowship, to the breaking of bread and the prayers. And awe came upon every soul, and many wonders and signs were being done through the apostles. And all who believed were together and had all things in common. And they were selling their possessions and belongings and distributing the proceeds to all, as any had need. And day by day, attending the temple together and breaking bread in their homes, they received their food with glad and generous hearts, praising God and having favor with all the people. And the Lord added to their number day by day those who were being saved." Acts 2: 42-47 ESV.

As foretold by Joel, a time of signs and wonders spread through the land while the believers grew in might and number. Stepping forth empowered by the very presence of the Father, the new believers walked forth their calling, living in community as one united by faith and salvation through the Messiah. Walking in newfound unity, they gathered with joyful and generous hearts, praising the One who had given His all and rose again in conquest over sin's grasp. Following in the steps of their beloved Savior, the new believers met daily in the temple, worshipping and living within the fullness of their Jewish heritage. While the community of believers grew with the dawn of each day, the entirety of the Father's plan remained partially veiled, a plan of redemption destined to extend to all.

Resounding through the ages and extended first to the Jew, the new covenant envelopes the heart of the Father, beating always for His people and longing for their return. Stretching forth through His Son, the Almighty offered a new relationship to those who believed, one which would allow a walk with the Father as in the days of creation. As our Savior burst forth from death's grip, victory unimaginable issued forth to those who believed, breaking all that bound and restoring relationships envisioned through the ages. Desiring always the entirety of our beings, the Father has poured into our very bodies the gift of His Holy Spirit, empowering, instructing, and offering freedom unmerited. While we as believers have been granted the Holy Spirit, the new covenant has not yet reached its fulfillment. All of creation groans, waiting in anticipation for His return and for a knowledge of our Father as yet inconceivable. A day rests just beyond our comprehension, a time when His law will be so fully inscribed upon our hearts that we will no longer struggle to obey, when we will know Him as never before innately within our spirits. Our hearts will one day beat in perfect time with His, pulsing in full recognition of the victory attained. The snares and cycle of sin will be forever shattered, and forgiveness granted to a depth previously unknown. One day Israel will dwell safely in her land, she will know the God of Israel, and she will remain as always His beloved. As creation groans, a loving Father waits in anticipation, yearning for all to return. While the book of Acts proceeds, the Father's initial promise to Abraham is further unveiled as His blessing pours forth to the nations.

17

Biblical History of Covenant
The Nations

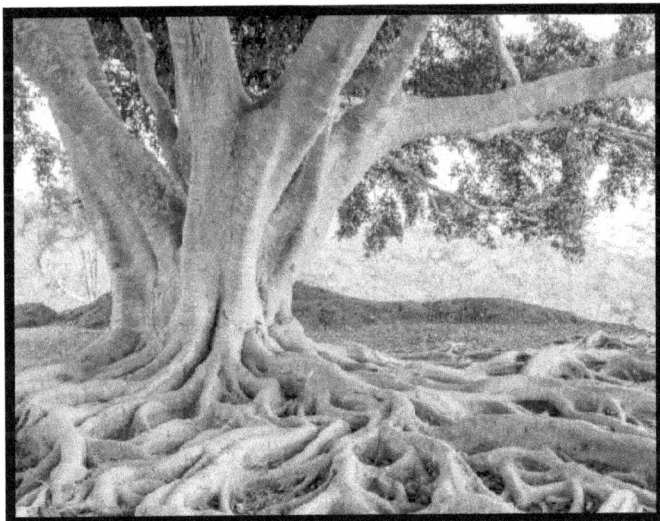

"At Caesarea there was a man named Cornelius, a centurion of what was known as the Italian Cohort, a devout man who feared God with all his household, gave alms generously to the people, and prayed continually to God. About the ninth hour of the day he saw clearly in a vision an angel of God come in and say to him, 'Cornelius.' And he stared at him in terror and said, 'What is it, Lord?' And he said to him, 'Your prayers and your alms have ascended as a memorial before God. And now send men to Joppa and bring one Simon who is called Peter. He is lodging with one Simon, a tanner, whose house is by the sea.'" Acts 10: 1-6 ESV.

"The next day, as they (those sent by Cornelius) were on their journey and approaching the city, Peter went up on the housetop about the sixth hour to pray. And he became hungry and wanted something to eat, but while they were preparing it, he fell into a trance and saw the heavens opened and something like a great sheet descending, being let down by its four corners upon the earth. In it were all kinds of animals and reptiles and birds of the air. And there came a voice to him: 'Rise, Peter; kill and eat,' But Peter said 'By no means, Lord; for I have never eaten anything that is common or unclean.' And the voice came to him a second time, 'What God has made clean, do not call common.' This happened three times, and the thing was taken up at once to heaven." Acts 10:9-16 ESV. Parenthetical note my own.

A meeting of divine importance had been ordained, a gathering destined to bring fulfillment to promises of old. Stretching forth through visions, the Lord moved within the spirits of Cornelius and Peter, drawing together those who would not have intimately gathered, a Jew and a gentile. Up unto this point, the work of the apostles had focused upon the Jewish communities. While gentiles were allowed some access to the temple and synagogues, the Jews did not dine with or enter the homes of a gentile out of a desire to remain ceremonially clean. While not forbidden in Scripture, Jewish history and interpretation prohibited the fellowshipping of Jews with gentiles to avoid possible contact with things or practices which were considered unclean. As the good news was preached throughout Judea and Samaria, the depth of the Father's plan and its implications outside the realm of Judaism remained just beyond the apostles' grasp. For a gentile to come to faith at this time, most believed a full conversion to Judaism, which included circumcision and strict adherence to Torah, was necessary. As Cornelius and Simon Peter prayed, the Father stretched forth and further unfolded His tapestry of redemption. As a Jew, Peter knew the commandments provided through the Torah, the rabbi's interpretations through the ages, and the unchanging nature of the Lord which would never ask that he violate Torah. As hunger stirred within, his spirit was opened to visions of food and a command destined to spread to the ends of the earth. After pondering the vision's meaning,

Peter understood that the animals within the vision symbolized gentiles who had been considered unclean. The Father moved within the spirit of Peter, yearning for him to grasp the true intent of His heart, to remember His promise to Abraham, to feel His longing for all nations. At that very moment, three gentiles stood at the door requesting Peter's presence and welcoming him to visit the home of a Roman centurion in Caesarea. With faith, Peter stepped forward and traveled to the home of Cornelius, unaware of the miracles to come. The heart of the Father longed for His creation, and an event which would forever change the impact of the good news yearned to burst forth.

"So Peter opened his mouth and said: 'Truly I understand that God shows not partiality, but in every nation anyone who fears him and does what is right is acceptable to him. As for the word that he sent to Israel, preaching good news of peace through Jesus Christ (he is Lord of all), you yourselves know what happened throughout all Judea, beginning from Galilee after the baptism that John proclaimed: how God anointed Jesus of Nazareth with the Holy Spirit and with power. He went about doing good and healing all who were oppressed by the devil, for God was with him. And we are witness of all that he did both in the country of the Jews and in Jerusalem. They put him to death by hanging him on a tree, but God raised him on the third day and made him to appear, not to all the people but to us who had been chosen by God as witnesses, who ate and drank with him after he rose from the dead. And he commanded us to preach to the people and to testify that he is the one appointed by God to be judge of the living and the dead. To him, all the prophets bear witness that everyone who believes in him receives forgiveness of sins through his name.' While Peter was still saying these things, the Holy Spirit fell on all who heard the word. And the believers from among the circumcised who had come with Peter were amazed, because the gift of the Holy Spirit was poured out even on the Gentiles. For they were hearing them speaking in tongues and extolling God...." Acts 10:34-46 ESV.

Within this scene, the Father's heart was laid bare as the fullness of His design unfurled. Wishing that all nations might be restored to the intimacy desired from creation's breath, the Holy Spirit fell upon a people not called by His name. As Peter and the Jews accompanying him watched in amazement, the miracles of Shavuot blew also upon the gentiles, filling them with the Holy Spirit. Standing within the house of Cornelius, Peter stood in violation of Jewish custom, as he obeyed the voice of the Father above the advice of men. Walking in faith and in obedience to the Father's calling, Peter tread amidst uncharted territory and witnessed the mighty hand of the Father as never before imagined. With meticulous intervention, the Father orchestrated an unlikely meeting to usher in a gift He longed to bestow. As He flowed through the house of Cornelius, revelations and mysteries resolved illuminated the hearts of those present. The thread of redemption woven through the ages emerged, revealing in entirety the Father's heart and desire for His creation. While Israel remained His chosen nation, the gentiles would also receive the redemption so lovingly offered. Through Abraham, all nations of the earth would be blessed.

As tongues of flame hovered upon the apostles during Shavuot, so the fire of the Holy Spirit spread throughout the surrounding areas. Bringing the gospel to the Jew first, the apostles traveled from town to town, teaching the risen Messiah and the redemption offered through His death and resurrection. Within Acts 15, conditions are outlined through which Jew and gentile might fellowship together and thrive in unity. Known as the fellowship laws, four regulations were established by the apostles as a minimum for the gentiles to follow within their midst.

In a letter written by the Jerusalem Council to the gentile believers in Antioch, we find: "For it has seemed good to the Holy Spirit and to us to lay on you no greater burden than these requirements: that you abstain from what has been sacrificed to idols, and from blood, and from what has been strangled, and from sexual immorality. If you keep yourself from these, you will do well. Farewell." Acts 15: 28-29 ESV. Adherence to these laws would allow the gentile believers to be welcomed into the Jewish homes and synagogues without danger of Torah and cleanliness violations.

While the numbers of believers grew, so also did the opposition. As the new believers followed in the dust of their leader, they embraced the Jewish traditions of their Savior, meeting in the synagogues and relishing the rich heritage into which they had been grafted. Rather than presenting a new religion called Christianity, congregations at this point looked undeniably Jewish. Flowing naturally forth from Jesus and the apostles, the gospel proclaimed throughout the land was grounded in Torah and displayed the perfect, unchanging nature of the Father. Tensions mounted within the Jewish communities between those who believed in Jesus' identity as the Messiah and those who remained blind to the truth.

"After this Paul left Athens and went to Corinth. And he found a Jew named Aquila, a native of Pontus, recently come from Italy with his wife Priscilla because Claudius had commanded all the Jews to leave Rome. ..." Acts 18: 1-2 ESV.

As pressures heightened, all the Jews were expelled from Rome during the reign of Claudius in approximately 49 AD, just sixteen years after the death of Christ. Suddenly, the gentile believers in Rome found themselves stripped of the foundations of their faith, struggling without the guidance of the patriarchs and the oracles which had passed through Jewish heritage. Because the new covenant had not yet been written, the fledgling believers were left with none who could fully interpret the Old Testament or uphold with accuracy the roots of their faith. At the time of the expulsion, thirteen synagogues were thriving within Rome, filled with Jews and Jewish and gentile believers.

When the Jews were allowed to return to Rome, the assemblies they encountered were vastly different from the congregations left just four years prior. It was to this scene that Paul addressed the book of Romans.

"They are Israelites, and to them belong the adoption, the glory, the covenants, the giving of the law, the worship, and the promises. To them belong the patriarchs, and from their race, according to the flesh, is the Christ, who is God over all, blessed forever. Amen." Romans 9:4-5 ESV.

Within the beginning pages of Genesis, a loving Father stretched forth, calling forward a man of righteousness displayed through belief. Through Abraham, a nation was meticulously crafted by the very hands of the Almighty, and a thread of redemption initiated. A nation would emerge, adopted as the Father's own and destined to proclaim His message throughout the earth. Chosen on the basis of faith, Abraham stepped forward into a future unknown, walking in obedience to the voice of the Father and unaware of the true implications to resound throughout time. Through Abraham would flow the adoption, glory, covenants, law, worship, promise, and the ultimate salvation offered to all. Even though Abraham had many sons, only one was chosen to carry the promise to the nations. While all remained valued equally in the eyes of the Father, only one was selected to deliver the covenants through the ages, forever changing the course of history and impacting the nations in ways inconceivable. Through Abraham, the Father crafted His nation, not because they were righteous on their own or numerous in size, but because they appeared instead small and insignificant. This fledgling nation would burst forth with a mission and calling irrevocable, displaying the power of the Almighty and proclaiming His name throughout the earth. It has always been through our weakness that the Father shines most brightly. Although the Jews were the first adopted sons of the Father, crafted with an anointing and covenant designed to bless the world, His message of redemption did not stop there. His has always been a heart desiring that all would know Him, that the nations would hear His call and receive the restoration He longed to impart.

"So I ask, did they stumble in order that they might fall? By no means! Rather through their trespass salvation has come to the Gentiles, so as to make Israel jealous. Now if their trespass means riches for the world, and if their failure means riches for the Gentiles, how much more will their full inclusion mean! But if some of the branches were broken off, and you, although a wild olive shoot, were grafted in among the others and now share in the nourishing root of the olive tree, do not be arrogant toward the branches. If you are, remember it is not you who support the root, but the root that supports you. Then you will say, 'Branches were broken off so that I might be grafted in.' That is true. They were broken off because of their unbelief, but you stand fast through faith. So do not become proud, but fear. For if God did not spare the natural branches, neither will he spare you. And even they, if they do not continue in their unbelief, will be grafted in, for God has the power to graft them in again. For if you were cut from what is by nature a wild olive tree, and grafted, contrary to nature, into a cultivated olive tree, how much more will these, the natural branches, be grafted back into their own tree." Romans 11: 11-12, 17-21, 23-24 ESV.

Set apart with distinctive values yet united with belief in Jesus, Jewish and gentile believers walk forward the callings issued from the breath of the Almighty. Although molded and crafted by His very hand, the Jewish nation as a whole stumbled, forgetting the calling for which she was designed. Destined to walk as a nation of priests illuminating the love and faithfulness of the Father, the nation chosen above all stumbled and was cut for a time from the cultivated olive tree because of unbelief. Though Israel has stumbled, she remains God's chosen nation with gifts and callings irrevocable and the ability to impact the world for Christ as no other. Through Israel's unbelief, salvation has flowed also to the gentiles, and we have been lovingly grafted into the olive tree of faith. While sharing belief in Christ, the gentiles carry a mission intertwined with the Jews yet distinct in purpose. Just as branches grafted into an olive tree retain their distinct appearance, so also do the branches of Jew and gentile believers display callings unique while stretching forth from a single tree. To usher in the fulfillment of His plan, both Jew and gentile believers are necessary, as each draw sustenance from the root of Truth while glorifying the One who made all. As God's treasured nation has wandered from her calling, the gentiles have been granted a mission of upmost importance, a calling to reach the Jews by provoking them to jealousy for the God of their forefathers and inspiring a return to their God. I wonder how we as Christians might fulfill our calling when we so little resemble the root which supports us, when we often overlook the Jewish nation and the people through whom the covenant has graciously flowed. While standing firm on the principles of salvation, how have we strayed so far from our roots, from that which supports our very salvation and from Whom we have been granted the opportunity to reside with the Father's chosen nation? Paul's warning rings hauntingly true. How the Father must grieve as He observes creation. How He must mourn that both Jew and gentile have largely forgotten their divine callings. A marvelous day looms upon the horizon when the Jewish nation will return to her God, when she will be grafted back into the olive tree and walk in the calling for which she was created. Yearning to rise above the skyline, the day waits in eager anticipation when Jewish and gentile believers will walk as one, unique in calling but unified in fulfilling the desires of His heart.

"He (Abraham) received the sign of circumcision as a seal of the righteousness that he had by faith while he was still uncircumcised. The purpose was to make him the father of all who believe without being circumcised, so that righteousness would be counted to them as well, and to make him the father of the circumcised who are not merely circumcised but who also walk in the footsteps of the faith that our father Abraham had before he was circumcised." Romans 4:11 ESV.

As the thread of redemption has flowed through history, the heart of the Father has stayed forever true, longing for all creation to repent and accept the gift so graciously offered. His is a heart desiring that none should perish but that all, Jew and gentile alike, receive the redemption extended. Long before prophets sounded through the land, the Father provided a glimpse of His meticulous plan, destined to impact the world in ways unimaginable and extend to the ends of the earth. As the new covenant flowed through the Jews to include the gentiles, Abraham would be called the spiritual father of both. Sustained by the beat of the Father's heart, Abraham's vitality pulsed in tune with the Father's, resulting in a life of faith.

The heart of the Father has beat always for the entirety of His creation, weaving continually a thread of redemption designed to flow also to the nations. As the people crafted by the Almighty's hands were delivered from bondage, multiples joined alongside sharing belief in the God of the Israelites and desiring to live as they. Through instructions granted to Moses and Aaron, a loving Father stretched forth and provided a path by which other nations might join in future Passover celebrations with the nation of Israel (Exodus 12: 48-49).

While His has always been a heart of inclusion, the beat

246

of distinction has also pulsed. Valuing and treasuring all equally, the Master has meticulously woven Israel and the nations together, desiring that neither lose their uniqueness and imparting each with a mission and calling for which they were designed. While the nation of Israel was chosen to carry the promise, the nations have retained equal importance. Without fulfillment of the missions granted to Jew and gentile, His ultimate desires remain incomplete. His is a heart of love, to Jew and gentile alike, valuing each equally and yearning that all would know Him. Desiring only belief and obedience flowing from love, He has stretched forth, creating each person purposefully and wonderfully, with a mission He longs to impart. To further reveal His heart for the entirety of creation, Ruth, a non-Jew, is included within the heritage of Jesus. Pausing and remembering the rich heritage of our faith allows the Father's true heart to beat within our beings, carrying a message of boundless devotion and inspiring a reverence for the Almighty previously unknown. While we as gentiles are not called to live as the Jews, we must remember the roots of our faith and the very foundation upon which our salvation rests. Contained within these roots lies richness unfathomable, nourishment like none other, and the true breath of the Father longing for His creation. Through belief and obedience, righteousness has always flowed. Set apart with distinctness and value, neither Jew nor gentile should boast, for their callings are not based upon their own merit but upon the divine will of the Father.

Wrapped within the words of Paul lies also the resounding theme of belief, a thread woven throughout the entirety of time. With unbelief, doubt, and disobedience, sin entered the world, severing relationship with our Father and threatening always to entrap. While gazing upon stars symbolizing the vastness of his offspring, Abraham believed the Lord, and it was counted to him as righteousness (Genesis 15:6). Capturing the intent of the law, Abraham believed prior to the written law and responded with obedience issuing forth from a devoted heart. With faith unwavering, Abraham knew within the core of his being that God was able to do all He had promised. From belief grew righteousness. Traversing into the New Testament, we find the standard unchanged. "But now the righteousness of God has been manifested apart from the law, although the Law and the Prophets bear witness to it – the righteousness of God through faith in Jesus Christ for all who believe. For there is no distinction: for all have sinned and fall short of the glory of God, and are justified by his grace as a gift, through the redemption that is in Christ Jesus." Romans 3:21-24.

Through Romans 11, Paul provides in vivid portrayal the consequences wreaked by unbelief as he entreats the new believers to walk humbly and steadfastly with faith. We should heed always the words of Paul, treading carefully upon the path of belief and guarding against any threat of distrust. Are we as Christians also filled with unbelief or distrust in the calling God has placed upon our lives? Have we strayed from that which

He has beckoned? Is our calling at times misdirected, and have we forgotten the roots which provide the very salvation and nourishment for our faith? Righteousness has always hinged upon faith; through belief has redemption flowed.

Echoing the words of the Father through the prophet Hosea, Paul recounted, "… Those who were not my people I will call 'my people', and her who was not beloved I will call 'beloved'. And in the very place where it was said to them, 'You are not my people.' There they will be called 'sons of the living God.'" Romans 9:25-26 ESV.

What a privilege to be called His people. What an honor to be grafted into the olive tree of faith, to receive the new covenant and the gift offered at a staggering cost. Let us remember always the rich heritage flowing forth from our Savior, Jesus the King of the Jews. Let us pause and reflect upon the true Cornerstone, the One upon Whom our salvation rests. Inhale the fullness of His heart, devotion, and design. Breathe in the entirety of His Word and the covenants woven through time, and draw sustenance from the Root which longs to support. "…. Remember it is not you who support the root, but the root that supports you." Romans11:18 ESV.

Tapestry Of Roots: Threads Woven By The Master

18

A Thread of Heritage
The Jewish Feasts and Festivals

"The Lord spoke to Moses, saying, 'Speak to the people of Israel and say to them, These are the appointed feasts of the Lord that you shall proclaim as holy convocations; they are my appointed feasts.'" Leviticus 23:1-2 ESV.

Through the words of Moses, the Lord breathed life into a nation crafted with His very hands and chosen above all peoples of the earth. Cognizant of the heart of man, He provided every assistance available to allow their success. Although the Israelites had walked with the Father as none before, the Lord was aware of the new nation's fragility and their innate tendency to forget the One who had provided their all. Desiring a love flowing forth from obedience, the Lord appointed specific feasts and festivals to serve as reminders of His faithfulness, summoning the Israelites to celebration, thanksgiving, and atonement. Within the words of Leviticus 23, Numbers 28 and 29, and Deuteronomy 16, the Lord established clear guidelines for His celebrations, including the dates, procedures, and offerings required. While seven major feasts were commanded, only three required all males to journey to Jerusalem for the festival. Although provided to the Jewish nation through the words of Moses, the feasts and festivals provided within these passages also carry significance and richness untold for all who share belief in Jesus. A thread of scarlet courses through each of the festivals illuminating the One destined to bring salvation to the nations and revealing the loving heart of a Father Who paid an inconceivable cost.

Emerging upon the plains stretching forth from the Jordan, the Israelites' radiated the protection and devotion of the Almighty. Set apart by their unique week comprised of seven days, their hearts beat in tune with their Father's, as they paused each week in remembrance of Him and displayed their covenantal sign of the Sabbath. Considered the most important feast, the Sabbath is celebrated at sundown every Friday and throughout the daylight hours on Saturday.

Wrapped within the words of Isaiah 53, we find portrayed the cornerstone of Christianity, the One destined to fulfill the promises of old in the most unlikely of ways. While hearts cried for immediate, physical release from worldly oppression, the

Father's plan of redemption was borne upon years of meticulous design and ways not of this earth. The words of the prophet, spoken centuries prior, illuminate the hope offered to all and capture the prophetic essence enveloped inside the Lord's festivals. Shining forth from the midst of each appointed feast was the fulfillment of His plan, the One born of a virgin destined to bear the iniquities of all to offer salvation to each.

"He was despised and rejected by men; a man of sorrows, and acquainted with grief; and as one from whom men hide their faces he was despised, and we esteemed him not.

Surely he has borne our griefs and carried our sorrows; yet we esteemed him stricken, smitten by God, and afflicted. But he was wounded for our transgressions; he was crushed for our iniquities; upon him was the chastisement that brought us peace, and with his stripes we are healed. All we like sheep have gone astray; we have turned – every one – to his own way; and the Lord has laid on him the iniquity of us all. He was oppressed, and he was afflicted, yet he opened not his mouth; like a lamb that is led to slaughter, and like a sheep that before its shearers is silent, so he opened not his mouth. By oppression and judgment he was taken away; and as for his generation, who considered that he was cut out of the land of the living, stricken for the transgression of my people? And they made his grave with the wicked and with a rich man in his death, although he had done no violence, and there was no deceit in his mouth." Isaiah 53: 3-9 ESV.

Passover, the Feast of Unleavened Bread, and the Feast of First Fruits

"The Lord said to Moses and Aaron in the land of Egypt, 'This month shall be for you the beginning of months. It shall be the first month of the year for you. Tell all the congregation of Israel that on the tenth day of this month every man shall take a lamb according to their fathers' houses, a lamb for a household. And you shall keep it until the fourteenth day of this month, when the whole assembly of the congregation of Israel shall kill their lambs at twilight. Then they shall take some of the blood and put it on the two doorposts and the lintel of the houses in which they eat it.'" Exodus 12:1-3, 6-7 ESV.

"And you shall observe the Feast of Unleavened Bread, for on this very day I brought your hosts out of the land of Egypt. Therefore you shall observe this day, throughout your generations, as a statute forever. In the first month, from the fourteenth day of the month at evening, you shall eat unleavened bread until the twenty-first day of the month at evening." Exodus 12:17-18 ESV.

In preparation for the birth of His nation, the Lord breathed instructions to His earthly leader, ushering in the deliverance and conception of a people treasured and chosen above all. Burdened by years of oppression, the Israelites' were likely incapable of comprehending the redemption approaching as they applied the lambs' blood to the doorposts and lintels of their dwellings. While the lamb was selected on the tenth day of the month of Nisan, it was not slaughtered until sundown of the fourteenth day, and they were instructed not to break any of its bones. After applying the covering of blood, the Israelites feasted upon lamb and unleavened bread before retiring. As they slept sheltered by the hand of the Almighty, the Lord struck down the firstborn of the Egyptians, allowing His path of redemption to burst forth. The Israelites hastened as release from bondage was granted and riches bestowed. While the Israelites journeyed, they continued to eat unleavened bread until the evening of the 21st day of Nisan, as instructed by the Lord. As the new nation stepped forth in independence and united by the hand of the Father, they were given the feasts of Passover and Unleavened Bread as remembrances of their mighty deliverance. These feasts comprise the first two major feasts of the spring season, and Passover marks the beginning of the Biblical year. A treasured nation chosen and crafted by the Almighty stepped forward into a future unknown and a calling to reach the nations.

"Now on the first day of Unleavened Bread the disciples came to Jesus, saying, 'Where will you have us prepare for you to eat the Passover?' He said, 'Go into the city to a certain man and say to him, The Teacher says, my time is at hand. I will keep the Passover at your house with my disciples.' And the disciples did as Jesus had directed them, and they prepared the Passover."

Matthew 26:17-19 ESV.

Commonly known as The Last Supper, the meal enjoyed by the disciples prior to Jesus' arrest was actually the Passover feast, held upon the first day of the celebration of Unleavened Bread. As they gathered in somber fellowship, another deliverance was foretold, one wrapped in sorrow and full of inconceivable repercussions. As events unfolded, a new covenant was unveiled and a cost of staggering proportions paid, allowing for the salvation of any who would accept. Through suffering unimaginable and grief unbearable, a loving Father stretched out to His creation and offered the ability to return to the fellowship for which they were created. In the midst of agony untold, He provided the pathway by which we might return to a freedom found only in Him and a way of life designed to allow prosperity and blessing. He had watched patiently as the thread of time traveled through history, carefully weaving a meticulous plan of redemption destined to bless the nations as promised to Abraham. If we would pause and reflect upon the ages past, we would see a devoted Father repeatedly displaying a heart of provision through countless experiences, words, and instruction. Desiring obedience and a love abounding therein, the Creator of all presented His Son as the Passover lamb, the covering by Whose blood all could be saved and by Whose scars all could be set free. Just as the blood of the innocent lamb covered the Israelites on the first Passover, so also does the blood of Jesus allow the salvation of all who believe. Though our precious Savior was beaten beyond recognition, His bones remained intact, just as the original Passover lamb. The feast practiced by the Israelites throughout the ages transpired in horrid reality, as our beloved Savior was crushed for our iniquities during the festival of Passover.

Through the feasts of Passover, Unleavened Bread, and First Fruits, we see the hand of a devoted Father stretching forth to humanity and offering to deal with the hold of sin upon our lives. Shining forth through the initial Passover instructions is the heart of a Father yearning to reconcile a relationship shattered by sin. As His words echoed through Moses, He longed to breathe new life into a people long oppressed but destined to carry His name. Wrapped within the initial Passover instructions, the Lord highlighted the problem of sin, or leaven, which separated the Israelites from their Father. Through the sacrifice of the lamb and the covering of blood upon their doorposts, He provided their deliverance and birth as a nation. As they walked forth from captivity, the Father lead faithfully through the waters of the Red Sea, as they were cleansed and empowered to commence the destiny for which they were created. What a beautiful portrayal and foreshadowing of what our Savior has done for us.

As we travel forward into the New Testament, we find Paul addressing the people of Corinth. "Your boasting is not good. Do you not know that a little leaven leavens the whole lump? Cleanse out the old leaven that you may be a new lump, as you really are unleavened. For Christ, our Passover lamb, has been sacrificed. Let us therefore celebrate the festival, not with the old leaven, the leaven of malice and evil, but with the unleavened bread of sincerity and truth." I Corinthians 5:6-8 ESV.

Speaking to a people familiar with the custom of

Passover, Paul longed to impart the true meaning of the festival to the believers. Strapped by the bonds of sin, we are utterly incapable of removing the sin which separates us from our Father and hinders the relationship we desire. Through the sacrifice of Christ and the covenant extended to all, the path by which we may return has been provided, orchestrated, and designed methodically from the beginning of time. Within the words of Paul, we find encouragement to walk in the victory which has been granted, to thrive under the devotion of a Father who has provided a way through an unfathomable cost. We are to walk in His truth, set free from the leaven which strives to bind and in full submission to the One who gave His absolute all.

Feast of First Fruits

Included within the Law provided through Moses, we find the words of Leviticus 23 and the origins of the next major feast of the Lord, the Feast of First Fruits. "Speak to the people of Israel and say to them, 'When you come into the land that I give you and reap its harvest, you shall bring the sheaf of the firstfruits of your harvest to the priest, and he shall wave the sheaf before the Lord, so that you may be accepted. On the day after the Sabbath the priest shall wave it. And you shall eat neither bread nor grain parched or fresh until this same day, until you have brought the offering of your God: it is a statute forever throughout your generations in all your dwellings.'" Leviticus 23:10-11, 14 ESV.

Enveloped within Passover and the Feast of Unleavened Bread is the Feast of First Fruits. Historically, the Israelites were instructed to give the first of everything to the Lord as a testimony of faith and thanksgiving for His provision. Contained within these instructions was the expectancy of trust, of giving to the Lord the first of their sustenance before partaking of any. According to Jewish tradition, this feast centered upon the barley harvest, and a field was grown and nurtured specifically for the festival. Following the Passover feast, the barley from the field was cut at sundown on the 15th of Nisan, and a crowd gathered in celebration on the 16th as the offering of First Fruits was presented to the Lord. As Jesus was sacrificed on Passover, He rose again at the approximate time of First Fruits, allowing those who had received the covenant to reap the benefits of a life renewed. The Feast of First Fruits is celebrated on the day after the Sabbath following Passover.

"I am the good shepherd. I know my own and my own know me, just as the Father knows me and I know the Father; and I lay down my life for the sheep. And I have other sheep that are not of this fold. I must bring them also, and they will listen to my voice. So there will be one flock, one shepherd. For this reason the Father loves me, because I lay down my life that I may take it up again. No one takes it from me but I lay it down of my own accord. I have authority to lay it down and I have authority to take it up again. This charge I have received from my Father." John 10:14-18 ESV.

While walking amidst the Pharisees, Jesus revealed a glimpse of the coming redemption and the mystery woven through time. Although eyes remained blind to the truth, Jesus spoke of one fold, of Jew and Gentile united under the care of the Shepherd who would pay the ultimate cost. As the good shepherd, Jesus walked upon the earth, nurturing, teaching, and guiding. Aware of the redemption coursing through his veins, He willingly offered His all, providing the atonement necessary to bring salvation to the nations. While others have been resurrected, only Christ has risen Himself. As Jesus rose again on First Fruits, the mystery was revealed, and a pathway uncovered by which all might be brought into the fold. Through Christ's death and resurrection, salvation and covenant could be extended to gentile also. As foretold in the Father's original covenant with Abraham, salvation was never intended to be exclusive to the Jew.

"But in fact Christ has been raised from the dead, the firstfruits of those who have fallen asleep. For as by a man came death, by a man has come also the resurrection of the dead. For as in Adam all die, so also in Christ shall all be made alive. But each in his own order: Christ the firstfruits, then at his coming those who belong to Christ." I Corinthians 15:20-23 ESV.

With arms outstretched in the midst of common criminals, Jesus offered His all, embodying the perfect Passover Lamb and the offering of first fruit. Through agony unimaginable,

He provided the ultimate sacrifice as the atonement for our transgressions, allowing a life renewed and a hope rebirthed to flow to those who would accept. With His death, all the sacrifices previously commanded within the Old Testament were fulfilled. Wrapped within the festival of First Fruits is the promise of more to come and the resurrection of those who believe. As Jesus exhaled His final breath upon the cross, the Father's plan was drawing to a close. The mighty veil tore within the temple, unveiling a plan woven from the beginning of time. With anticipation, the Father waited as the journey was completed. As Christ rose on the third day, a design woven through the ages burst forth, crushing the enemy and ushering in a victory which would reign forever.

The feasts of Passover, Unleavened Bread, and First Fruits call to remembrance the faithfulness of a Father, the ultimate cost of our transgressions, and the salvation provided through the blood of the Lamb. Within the Jewish calendar, the 14th of Nisan and the feast of Passover fluctuate continually. As recorded in Scripture, the Feast of First Fruits is celebrated on the day following the Sabbath after Passover, which would be Sunday. During the year of Jesus' crucifixion, the 14th of Nisan and Passover would have fallen on either a Wednesday or Thursday, and He rose on the following Sunday, which would have been the Feast of First Fruits.   When compared to our current calendar, the month of Nisan contains portions of March and April, and First Fruits occurs roughly around the time the church celebrates Easter. The Passover meal ushers in the Feast of Unleavened Bread, during which time no leaven is eaten for a period of seven days. During the Passover meal, the Israelite heritage is recounted, calling to remembrance the bitterness of slavery and the deliverance provided by the Father. With the Feast of Unleavened Bread sin is confronted, and within Passover and First Fruits rests our salvation.

Shavuot (Pentecost)

"You shall count seven full weeks from the day after the Sabbath, from the day that you brought the sheaf of the wave offering. You shall count fifty days to the day after the seventh Sabbath. Then you shall present a grain offering of new grain to the Lord." Leviticus 23:15-16 ESV.

The Feast of First Fruits commences the counting of days to the next festival prescribed by the Lord: Shavuot. To the ancient Israelite, this corresponded with the beginning of the yearly wheat harvest. Leading up to Shavuot, the Jewish nation would count the omer, which was a measurement of a sheaf of barley, for 49 consecutive days, and they thereafter provided the first wheat offering on the 50th day. As one of the major festivals, all males were required to present themselves before God in Jerusalem on this celebration. Jewish tradition thereafter connects Shavuot to the giving of the Law to Moses on Mount Sinai.

Traveling forward to the New Testament, we find an added dimension to the ancient festival of Shavuot, another aspect of a plan devised with creation's breath. Within Shavuot, we see the heartbeat of the Father, as He yearns to draw ever closer to His people and reside within their spirits. With meticulous design, the Father poured forth his Spirit upon the apostles on the day of Shavuot.

Prior to His death, Jesus spoke with the disciples, providing comfort and assurance for events they could not yet comprehend.

"If you love me, you will keep my commandments. And I will ask the Father, and he will give you another Helper, to be with you forever, even the Spirit of truth, whom the world cannot receive, because it neither sees him nor knows him. You know him, for he dwells with you and will be in you.

I will not leave you as orphans; I will come to you. Yet a little while and the world will see me no more, but you still see me. Because I live, you also will live. ..... But the Helper, the Holy Spirit, whom the Father will send in my name, he will teach you all things and bring to your remembrance all that I have said to you." John 15-19, 26 ESV.

As the disciples gazed in horror upon the cross, they were blind to the coming glory and the blessing cloaked within such tragedy. Although they had walked with Jesus as no other, they failed to truly grasp the Father's heart beating within His Son. Unsatisfied to be merely within our physical midst, the Father longed to reside within our very beings, to fill our entire essence with His love, protection, and perfect provision.

"When the day of Pentecost arrived, they were all together in one place. And suddenly there came from heaven a sound like a mighty rushing wind, and it filled the entire house where they were sitting. And divided tongues of fire appeared to them and rested on each one of them. And they were all filled with the Holy Spirit and began to speak in other tongues as the Spirit gave them utterance." Acts 2:1-4 ESV.

Ten days after Christ's ascension, the apostles gathered in celebration for the Feast of Shavuot when the inconceivable descended. While the indwelling of the Spirit had been foretold, none could have imagined the scene which transpired or the repercussions contained therein. With tongues of flames, the mighty hand of the Father stretched forth and instilled within them the Helper spoken of by Jesus, the One who would dwell within their beings, reminding them of the Father's words and offering an intimacy rarely encountered since the days of Adam. With the indwelling of the Spirt is re-birth, power, restoration of relationship, and the ability to walk as the Father would desire.

As the meaning wrapped within Shavuot has magnified from the wheat harvest to the giving of the Law to the conveying of the Holy Spirit, the Father has remained forever faithful, yearning always to impart more of Himself.   With the Law provided on Mount Sinai, the Father longed to reveal to the Israelites His true nature and the utter impossibility of living on their own as He would desire. With the giving of the Holy Spirit, He has placed His law upon our hearts and provided the power necessary to walk in the obedience He desires. Through the Holy Spirit, we are enabled to reside in the victory granted at the cross and feel the breath of the Father within our beings. If we would pause the busyness of our days and listen to that still, quiet voice, we would learn to walk in a power unbelievable and offered at a staggering cost.

The Feast of Trumpets, Rosh Hashanah

"And the Lord spoke to Moses, saying, 'Speak to the people of Israel, saying, In the seventh month, on the first day of the month, you shall observe a day of solemn rest, a memorial proclaimed with blast of trumpets, a holy convocation. You shall not do any ordinary work, and you shall present a food offering to the Lord.'" Leviticus 23:23-25 ESV.

The Feast of Trumpets begins the season of fall festivals prescribed by the Lord and commences the High Holidays in Jewish tradition. Established as the first of Tishri on the Jewish calendar, this festival served as a period of preparation for the upcoming Yom Kippur. As the Israelites blew the shofar, or ram's horn, in celebration, they entered into a time of introspection and remembrance. As rabbinical history continued, the Feast of Trumpets expanded into the celebration of the New Year, as the rabbis connected the first of Tishri to the creation of humanity. The month of Tishri corresponds to portions of September and October in our current calendar.

"But we do not want you to be uninformed, brothers, about those who are asleep, that you may not grieve as others do who have no hope. For since we believe that Jesus died and rose again, even so, through Jesus, God will bring with him those who have fallen asleep. For this we declare to you by a word from the Lord, that we who are alive, who are left until the coming of the Lord, will not precede those who have fallen asleep. For the Lord himself will descend from heaven with a cry of command, with the voice of an archangel, and with the sound of the trumpet of God. And the dead in Christ will rise first. Then we who are alive, who are left, will be caught up together with them in the clouds to meet the Lord in the air, and so we will always be with the Lord. Therefore encourage one another with these words." I Thessalonians 4:13-18 ESV.

Within the Feast of Trumpets rests hope and a glimpse of the glory to come for all who believe in Jesus. Throughout Jewish history, trumpets have been used as a call to assemble for worship, feast, festival, or battle. At the sound of trumpets, the Almighty's judgment upon Jericho burst forth, just as they will one day release judgments upon the earth. While storms swirl and wickedness threatens, we rest in the assurance of things unseen and the heart of a Father desiring that none should perish. With trumpet blast, Jesus will one day descend upon the clouds, resurrecting those who have passed before and bringing forth those called by His name. As He appears in full glory and might, a victory long ago achieved will at once be fully realized. As the Father's thread weaves through history, the tapestry is woven and the plan unveiled, producing the victory bought at a cost unfathomable and restoring relationships desired since the breath of creation.

Yom Kippur, the Day of Atonement

"And the Lord spoke to Moses, saying, 'Now on the tenth day of this seventh month is the Day of Atonement. It shall be for you a time of holy convocation, and you shall afflict yourselves and present a food offering to the Lord. And you shall not do any work on that very day, for it is a day of atonement, to make atonement for you before the Lord your God.'" Leviticus 23:26-28 ESV.

"And this shall be a statute forever for you, that atonement may be made for the people of Israel once in the year because of all their sins ...." Leviticus 16:34 ESV.

After the blowing of the shofar on the first of Tishri, the Israelites approached the Day of Atonement with an air of repentance. Commencing at sundown on the night of the ninth, they prayerfully entered a somber day of rest, fasting, and seeking forgiveness. Remembered as the holiest day of the Jewish calendar, Yom Kippur was the day on which the high priest made atonement for the nation of Israel. After somber preparation, the high priest entered the Holy of Holies and uttered the name of the Father known only to him at the prescribed time each year, adorned with a rope attached to his body. In the event that he failed to be ceremonially clean or the sacrifice was found lacking, the rope would allow the priest's body to be extracted without anyone else entering the sanctuary. The Israelites waited outside in anticipation, hopeful the rope would prove unnecessary. As the high priest sprinkled the blood of the goat upon the mercy seat, the atonement was complete.

Wrapped within Yom Kippur is the ceremony of the scapegoat, during which the high priest symbolically laid the sins of the Israelites upon the head of a goat prior to its release into the wilderness. After completing the sin offering for himself and family, the high priest would take from the congregation of Israel two goats to be used as a sin offering for the nation. Placing the goats before the Lord at the tent of meeting, lots were then cast which would determine which of the goats was set apart as a sacrifice for the Lord. Once atonement had been made for the nation of Israel, the high priest then laid hands upon the remaining goat, confessing the transgressions of the nation and releasing the animal to then bear the iniquities to a land removed. Even though one goat had already been sacrificed for the sins of the people, the Lord provided the ceremony of the scapegoat, indicating that true redemption could not be accomplished through the blood of goats or bulls. Prior to the goat's release, a piece of red wool was attached to the animal's head, and an interesting phenomenon emerged. While Jewish tradition reports that the wool would often turn to white, years also passed during which the wool remained red. While the blood of an animal was at that time required for atonement, it would not always be thus, as the perfect Lamb would one day bear the cost of all iniquity.

Within the festival of Yom Kippur we see a beloved Savior stretched upon a rudimentary cross, enduring suffering unimaginable to bring the atonement required. A plan woven from the beginning of time displayed a tapestry of redemption, unveiling the heart of a Father longing for His creation. As scarred hands stretched forth, an offer unfathomable was extended, allowing salvation for all who believe and the opportunity to walk with the Father as envisioned through the ages. Just as the mighty veil within the temple split at the time of Jesus' death, so also has the sin separating us from the Father been severed, allowing entrance into the Holy of Holies and the ability to again dwell intimately with the Father. Upon a cross of wood, our Savior poured forth his life and fulfilled the sacrificial requirements for all time.

When reviewing Jewish history through the Talmud, beautiful symbolism shines forth through the ceremony of the scapegoat. As a compilation of rabbinic oral tradition relating to the Law, the Babylonian Talmud was assembled throughout the third to fifth centuries and was completed approximately 500 AD.

Within Tractate Yoma, chapter 4 of the Babylonian Talmud, we find, "The rabbis taught: Forty years before the Temple was destroyed, the lot never came into the right hand, the red wool did not become white, the western light did not burn, and the gates of the Temple opened of themselves, till the time that R. Johanan b. Zakkai rebukcd them, saying: "Temple, Temple, why alarmest thou us? We know that thou art destined to be destroyed. For of thee hath prophesied Zechariah ben Iddo [Zech. xi. 1]: 'Open thy doors, O Lebanon, and the fire shall eat thy cedars.'" [9]

Enveloped within this ancient rabbinical text is the hint of a mystery unknown to the original writers, which began in the year 30 AD, the approximate year in which our Messiah died and forty years before the temple was destroyed. As the Jewish nation witnessed Yom Kippur each year and conducted the ceremony of the scapegoat, they faithfully attached a piece of crimson wool to the head of the scapegoat. Interestingly, throughout the period of forty years after the death of Jesus and before the destruction of the temple, the lot for the Lord

---

[9] Jewishvirtuallibrary.org, accessed October 4, 2015.

never came into the priest's right hand, and the red wool did not turn white. Against all statistical probability, these two events continued year after year, revealing the heart of a Father longing to impart the true meaning of Jesus' death. In spite of His absolute all, the heartbeat of the Father and the ultimate plan of redemption remained misunderstood.

"For Christ has entered, not into holy places made with hands, which are copies of the true things, but into heaven itself, now to appear in the presence of God on our behalf. Nor was it to offer himself repeatedly, as the high priest enters the holy places every year with blood not his own, for then he would have had to suffer repeatedly since the foundation of the world. But as it is, he has appeared once for all at the end of the ages to put away sin by the sacrifice of himself." Hebrews 9:24-26 ESV.

With the death and resurrection of Jesus, a new covenant would be offered, one inscribed upon our very hearts and destined to reach the ends of the earth. Envisioned within Yom Kippur is the embodiment of the high priest and sacrifice combined and fulfilled through the atoning blood of Christ.

Feast of Booths (Tabernacles) / Sukkot

"And the Lord spoke to Moses, saying, 'Speak to the people of Israel, saying, On the fifteenth day of this seventh month and for seven days is the Feast of Booths to the Lord. On the first day shall be a holy convocation; you shall not do any ordinary work. For seven days you shall present food offerings to the Lord. On the eighth day you shall hold a holy convocation and present a food offering to the Lord. It is a solemn assembly; you shall not do any ordinary work.'" Leviticus 23:33-36 ESV.

"And they found it written in the Law that the Lord had commanded by Moses that the people of Israel should dwell in booths during the feast of the seventh month, and that they should proclaim it and publish it in all their towns and in Jerusalem, 'Go out to the hills and bring branches of olive, wild olive, myrtle, palm, and other leafy trees to make booths, as it is written.' ….. They kept the feast seven days, and on the eight day there was a solemn assembly, according to the rule." Numbers 8:14-15, 18.

After passing through the waters of the Red Sea, the Israelites emerged as a new people, crafted and empowered by the Almighty. A fledgling nation long oppressed walked forward into a future unknown but lead by the One who had wrought a deliverance bursting with signs and wonders. Desiring to reveal more of Himself, He resided within their midst, providing every need and guiding through cloud and flame. The Israelites lived with the visible, daily presence of the Father not experienced since the days of creation. As chains of affliction were cast aside, renewed life from the Father was inhaled as they embarked upon a destiny yet unknown. Prior to the written Law, the Almighty dwelled within their very midst, yearning to reveal the beat of His heart and the depth of His devotion. As the Israelites traveled through the wilderness, they remained completely dependent upon the Father for their absolute all, their source of sustenance, protection, and direction.

Knowing that time dims memories once vivid, the Father provided a yearly festival in remembrance of the sacred time spent with the Israelites in the wilderness. As the Festival of Booths was celebrated each fall, the Israelites were reminded of the One who met their every need, Who provided a deliverance unimaginable and a devotion immeasurable. Dwelling in tents for eight days, they were reminded of the time the Lord resided and traveled visibly within their midst, always near and forever faithful. The Festival of Booths is the last major harvest festival of the year and the third major feast requiring the males to travel to Jerusalem. Celebrated in the month of Tishri (September or October), the Festival of Booths also correlates most closely to the birth of Jesus, when the Father again chose to dwell visibly amongst His people.

Just as the Israelites' time in the wilderness was fleeting, so also is this life temporary. Dwelling in tents or shelters of limbs, we are reminded today of the transitory nature of this earth and of our true home one day with the Father. Longing always to edge ever closer to His creation, the Almighty stretched forth through the body of Jesus and offered the opportunity to walk with Him as never before. Within the new covenant lies the promise of a Helper, the presence of the Holy Spirit dwelling within our very beings. Previously, the Holy Spirit had been granted only for specific times and purposes. While the Lord provided the Law, the empowerment to live as desired was not conferred until the permanent indwelling of the Holy Spirit. With the immersion of the Holy Spirit, we are granted the empowerment to obey. As the Israelites celebrated the Feast of Booths, they remembered a time when their Father dwelled within their very midst, a time which would again come to pass as Jesus walked the earth. Today, while believers are instilled with the Holy Spirit, we long for the return of our Messiah, when He will again be visibly within our midst. The Master's story weaves through history with threads of faithfulness, grace, and provision. He stands forever near, longing for us to grasp His true nature, to feel the beat of His heart within our bodies, and to seize the breath of deliverance purchased at a price unthinkable.

Through the feasts of the Lord flows the thread of grace, defined as kindness unmerited and power granted. Within the harvest festivals of First Fruits, Shavuot, and Feast of Booths, as well as the Passover, we see the unwarranted grace of the Father extended through provision and absolute care. Enveloped within the feasts of Passover, Unleavened Bread, Feast of Trumpets, and the Day of Atonement, we are reminded of our sinful nature and need for a Savior. Shining forth through these festivals is the gift of salvation, offered to the unworthy at a staggering cost. Within Shavuot, we see the secondary meaning of grace, as empowerment through the Holy Spirit is granted to all who accept the gift of salvation and covenant offered.

Within the Feasts of the Lord, a three-fold cord weaves, strong and worthy of remembrance, abounding in implications, and illustrating the entirety of the Master's plan. While the thread of festivals intertwines through history, it is joined inextricably with grace and the image of Jesus. Through the feasts and festivals, the heart of the Father is laid bare, yearning for the restoration of relationships and revealing the method by which favor may be bestowed. As grace flows forth, we see a kindness and favor undeserved and an empowerment unimaginable. Held within sin's grasp, humanity battles continually to submit fully to the One providing our very breath, struggling forevermore with our inability to meet His desires with our own merit. As such, we breathe dependent upon His grace, favor undeserved and unwarranted, and we walk daily with the grace of empowerment provided through the Holy Spirit. How the Father longs for us to grasp every aspect of His nature, to embrace Jesus within the context of His heritage and to hold in esteem the feasts ordained. Wrapped within the feasts, His story of redemption and empowerment shines through, unlocking the mystery of time and the heart of a Father yearning for His creation.

19

The True Gospel

"Now as they were eating, Jesus took the bread, and after blessing it broke it and gave it to the disciples, and said, 'Take, eat; this is my body.' And he took a cup, and when he had given thanks he gave it to them saying, 'Drink of it, all of you, for this is my blood of the covenant, which is poured out for the many for the forgiveness of sins.'" Matthew 26:26-28 ESV.

Ours is a God of covenants. As time has coursed through ages past, a loving Father has stayed forever near, longing always for relationship and devotion flowing forth from the hearts of His creation. As His breath flowed through the nostrils of Adam, a new life was created, a life intertwined with hope and choice. Although He knew the events which would unfold, the Almighty exhaled the breath of life and offered a walk with Him, a trust unfathomed, and a choice. Without choice, true love does not exist. While the ultimate cost of this offer would be staggering, our beloved Father stretched forth with devotion and hope, desiring a relationship based upon choice and obedience issuing forth from a desire for Him. At the core of our very existence lies a need for relationships, with our Father and with those walking along our paths. As sin and distrust slithered forth onto the earth and within the heart of man, the relationship coveted from the breath of creation was severed. While His heart grieved in the face of rebellion and distrust, hope was never lost. Instead, a plan was initiated, an arrangement of miraculous proportions destined to cover the entirety of the earth. Contrary to worldly design, our Heavenly Father responded not with forced obedience but instead with an offer of His Son, again honoring choice above coercion. Operating upon a plane vastly opposed to the ways of the world, He stretched forth in trustworthiness and leadership foreign to human nature. Wrapped within the design beat the true heart of the Father beckoning a return to fellowship and yearning that all would know Him. How He must long for us to truly inhale His breath, to trust within our very core that His intent for us is always for our good. Always.

Aspiring relationships and obedience above all, the Almighty has stretched forth throughout time and spoken within the context of covenants. Through covenants, His very spirit is understood and a template provided by which we may enter into the relationship He so desires. While a covenant is typically understood as an agreement, its true essence is enveloped within the underlying relationship, the purpose for which the covenant was established. For a covenant to be received, it must first be offered. While various types of covenants exist, acceptance of the agreement ordinarily necessitates conditions and stipulations designed to maintain the relationship, allowing full benefits of the agreement to flow to both parties. Within the stipulations, conditions often outline blessings for obedience and consequences for indiscretions. Once all the conditions have been accepted and the boundaries of the relationship established, a sign is customarily provided to serve as a call to remembrance through the ages. While the covenant of salvation is known as a kingly grant requiring only belief on the part of the recipient, acceptance of the covenant necessitates action thereafter. Obedience must ensue. Although a free gift, the true cost of salvation is absolutely all, for you must daily submit your desires to that of your Father's and walk in tune with His breath. As Jesus laid down his life for the many, so must the believer lay down his own, forgoing his very flesh for Him who makes all and provides so abundantly. Through belief has righteousness always flowed. Obedience issuing forth from a heart devoted has been His language of love for all time. Walking with the disciples, Jesus said "If you love me, you will keep my commandments." John 14:15 ESV. His thread of redemption has coursed through ages past and present, meticulously woven through covenants so that we might grasp the beat of His heart, inhale the breath of life, and receive the deliverance He longs to impart. Wrapped within a covenant lies the Cornerstone of salvation, the relationship extended by the Creator of all to a creation unworthy. To miss the context of covenant is to miss the beat of His heart, a heart beating and yearning for all to know and receive the relationship offered at a cost unfathomable. With belief comes responsibility, not within the terms of works based righteousness, but a heart change where obedience issues forth naturally from a heart devoted and surrendered. As the covenant is accepted, the sign of the Holy Spirit flows forth, providing the empowerment to obey and the ability to live as He would desire. Not content to merely guide through scripture or walk alongside, the Father would now dwell within man's very being.

In spite of covenants extended and devotion inconceivable, the true heart of our Father has often remained just beyond grasp. From creation's breath, a heart mighty and full has stretched forth, offering relationship and devotion pure wrapped within the ability to choose. As new life filled the lungs of Adam, free will coursed through his veins, providing a decision upon which the fate of humanity balanced. Knowing the choice would ultimately go awry, the Almighty still created, still hoped, still waited with baited breath, still provided to man that which he would desire above all but would ultimately bring death and destruction. A choice was necessary. Choose to believe in the good and perfect will of the Father or distrust and follow the desires of the human heart. Submission or self-rule. With choice crept the allure of sin, slithering and suggesting that perhaps God was withholding something wondrous from His creation, that perhaps He didn't truly desire the best for all, and that perhaps man might in his humanity know better. In reality, His heart's desire was to protect us from our very beings. Walking with Adam in the Garden, the Almighty's heart beat in fullness, yearning for man to feel the pulse of His heart and the breath which brought forth life, longing that man would grasp His devotion, that he would choose to believe his Creator above the whisperings stirring within. Because there must be a choice, one law was provided. How the Father must have grieved as the errant choice became reality, bringing that which He foreknew to fruition. Although Adam walked in harmony unimaginable, the stirrings of distrust within brought forth disobedience and a fatal choice to walk from under the full submission required by the Almighty. How we have misunderstood His heart. From here stems the essence of our issue - our sinful desire to indulge and follow ourselves rather than submit to the One who provides our very all.

"Hear, O Israel: the Lord our God, the Lord is one. You shall love the Lord your God with all your heart and with all your soul and with all your might. And these words that I command you today shall be upon your heart. You shall teach them diligently to your children, and shall talk of them when you sit in your house and when you walk by the way, and when you lie down, and when you rise. You shall bind them as a sign on your hand, and they shall be as frontlets between your eyes. You shall write them on the doorposts of your house and on your gates." Deut. 6:4-9 ESV.

As the thread of time traveled forward, sin and wickedness progressed, necessitating the need for additional laws to illuminate transgressions and the need for redemption. Stretching forth to a creation bursting with rebellion, a loving Father provided the Law and conditions through which relationships with Him might be restored. With each beat of His heart, the Father desires His creation, longing for them to know the depths of His character, the intent of His heart, and the importance of obedience flowing forth from a desire for Him. As Paul spoke to the new believers and communities throughout the surrounding lands, he brought repeated assurance that the Law was good. (1 Tim 1:8, Romans 7:12). In addition to providing the will of God, the Law brings to mind our sins, holds us accountable, and provides protection as we walk our earthly paths. As the passage of time weaves days into centuries, the Law remains unchanged, reflecting the steadfast, sure nature of our Father and beckoning submission true and pure. The Law provided by the Father stands perfect, unchanged by the passage of time, and reflects underlying heart principles with moral and relational implications designed to foster health amongst His people.

If we would pause momentarily and inhale the true breath of our Father, we would find the arms of grace enveloping and permeating the Law provided for our good. While grace may be defined as unmerited favor or an undeserved gift, it is also the empowerment to obey. With the gift of the Holy Spirit, we are provided the permanent presence of the Almighty providing the ability to walk in obedience to His desires. Through the Law, our inability to live as He desires is manifest, and our need for grace and redemption is revealed. Without the unmerited gift of grace, which is exhibited through the Law, we cannot receive the salvation and the grace flowing forth as empowerment which He longs to deliver. The two, grace and law, are inextricably entwined. In the absence of one, the true meaning of the other passes unfulfilled.

As the offer of the New Covenant is accepted, His laws begin to be inscribed upon our hearts and the Holy Spirit is granted, providing a change within our beings and the ability to live as He would desire. Rather than altering His expectations, He graciously allows a change within our very core. While the covenant flows through belief, action must ensue, bringing forth a following and submission to the One who gave His all. A loving Father stands forever near, waiting patiently for all to follow and yearning for devotion stemming from a heart true and submitted to His Kingdom. He desires a heart change, a bride, one who chooses obedience of his own heart volition rather than a mere outward obedience to stipulations. While the rules remain the same, our heart is forever changed in ways undeserving and unfathomable. Echoing the words of the Almighty, Jesus said, "If you love me, you will keep my commandments." John 14:15 ESV. Loving God requires obedience. To obey, you must first know the expectations. Through the gift of the Holy Spirit comes the ability to obey through grace, which is defined as the empowerment to obey and the unmerited gift.

"In those days, John the Baptist came preaching in the wilderness of Judea, 'Repent, for the kingdom of heaven is at hand.'" Matthew 3:1-2 ESV.

"Now when he heard that John had been arrested, he withdrew into Galilee. And leaving Nazareth he went and lived in Capernaum by the sea, in the territory of Zebulun and

Naphtali, so that what was spoken by the prophet Isaiah might be fulfilled:

'The land of Zebulum and the land of Naphtali, the way of the sea, beyond the Jordan, Galilee of the Gentiles – the people dwelling in darkness have seen a great light, and for those dwelling in the region and shadow of death, on them a light has dawned.'

From that time Jesus began to preach, saying, 'Repent, for the kingdom of heaven is at hand.'" Matthew 4:12-17 ESV.

As redemption's thread traversed into the New Testament, the Master's tapestry was further revealed. A plan woven through the ages transformed into vivid reality, bringing a message destined to impact the world as no other. Weaving this thread throughout the loom of time stands a loving Father in pursuit of His creation, yearning for relationships envisioned with creation's breath. As the voice of John the Baptist resounded through the wilderness, so Jesus also spoke forth calling all to repentance. Within this one word lies the true message of the gospel. Repent. In Hebrew, repent is defined as turning back or away, denoting an action and effort. With the first errant choice, sin slithered into the heart of humanity, binding and deceiving the heart designed to pulse in tune with its Creator. While the Hebrew meaning of sin is an offense, the Greek definition recounts missing the mark, the holiness of God. All sin finds itself rooted in disobedience to God, missing the mark of His holiness and choosing to follow the desires of our own hearts rather than our Creator. Ours is God, holy and pure, Who demands a staggering perfection and heart devotion from His people, a perfection of which we are fully incapable. Once the depravity of our condition is realized, a repentance and turning away from a prior life of sin and self-rule must ensue. We must lay down our life, our will, and our desire to be in control, relinquishing every aspect of our being to the Almighty. Believing in the presence, person, and resurrection of our Messiah, we must repent of a life of sin and self-enthronement, a life lived contingent upon our own desires and void of the One who pursues. Daily, we must turn from that which strives to entangle and submit fully to the One who paid the ultimate cost and brought redemption to a world unworthy. Capturing the essence of repentance, Paul spoke to the church in Galatia, "I have been crucified with Christ. It is no longer I who live, but Christ who lives in me. And the life I now live in the flesh I live by faith in the Son of God, who loved me and gave himself for me." Galatians 2:20 ESV.

"Repent, for the kingdom of heaven is at hand." Matthew 4:17 ESV. As the very presence of God walked on earthly soil, His heart called forth, yearning for reconciliation and beckoning all to repentance. Rather than presenting a standard plan of salvation common to all, He reached out to each person, pinpointing with precision that which would be the crux of their salvation. Whether speaking to Nicodemus, the woman at the well, or the rich young ruler, Jesus met all within their circumstances and revealed the area they most longed to hold with fists clenched, the area preventing total submission and full repentance. Where Adam and Eve erred, so have we. Whisperings stirring within have called into question the motives of our Father, urging the separation of areas within our spirits where we retain control. As the words echo through time, He longs for us to truly hear, to inhale the breath He longs to impart and respond with a heart fully submitted and trusting in His good and perfect will. Desiring a relationship with us deep and true, He stretches forth, longing to free us from ourselves and the temptations which so easily ensnare. While our fleshly desire for control brings death and decay, repentance births freedom inconceivable.

With the acceptance of the New Covenant, a relationship is established, lovingly offered through the atonement of Jesus while we remained yet enslaved by sin. An opportunity to live in relationship with our Father, the Creator of all, full of majesty, glory, and holiness, has been granted to the least of us. How can such a privilege be treated lightly? The Creator of the universe, our very beings, our breath, waits patiently with outstretched arms, yearning that we would grasp the intent of His heart and the covenant extended through scarred hands. How He longs for relationship full and perfect, abounding from hearts choosing obedience and submission to His perfect will. Hearts desiring within their innermost recesses to live fully for Him is His greatest desire. While sin has swirled and wickedness bound, He has remained forever near pursuing His creation, weaving a tapestry of redemption through which we might return. He has watched, waited, planned, and pursued. He longs to reside within our very beings, to provide again the breath of our existence. The cost of the call is repentance.

"Do not think that I have come to abolish the Law or the Prophets; I have not come to abolish them but to fulfill them. For truly, I say to you, until heaven and earth pass away, not an iota, not a dot, will pass from the law until all is accomplished." Matthew 5:17-18 ESV.

As the feet of our beloved Savior tread upon earthly shores, He yearned for all to grasp the mission to which He was called, a mission of freedom and deliverance foretold by the prophets and intricately entwined with the Law. Bringing fulfillment to words spoken centuries prior, Jesus brought the heart of the Father wrapped within a cloak of humanity. Enveloped within the folds beat the pulse of the Almighty, offering an understanding of the true intent of the Law and a restoration inconceivable. As Jesus walked with the disciples, He confirmed the unchanging nature of the Almighty and offered the deeper implications held within the recesses of words spoken throughout time. Once we accept the salvation offered, however, our responsibility does not stop, for we have entered into a covenant with our Creator. A relationship has been established, a relationship requiring true, full submission and obedience to our Heavenly Father. While the offer is free, the cost is our absolute all. Within a covenant are rules and stipulations designed to sustain the relationship and protect against the evil stirrings within. Calling all to repentance, the essence of His invitation is submission, an offer to walk in His ways with the power and guidance of the Holy Spirit. While we are in Him a new creation, old natures strive to ensnare, and we must learn always to abide fully in the One who gave His all. We must walk daily in true repentance and submission, allowing our hearts to beat in unity with the perfect will of our Father.

If we would pause momentarily and inhale the enormity of the covenant accepted, how our daily walk with the Almighty might transform. Abiding fully in Him releases the calling for which we were designed and the victory and power bought at a cost unimaginable. Searching for the restoration only He can provide, a world replete with chaos and death awaits the Master's call. Let us listen to His voice, abide fully in His will, and walk forth with the victory attained at the cross and longing to reach the ends of the earth. The cost of our redemption is too high and the offer too grand to be received with flippant word and deed.

"Then Jesus went with them to a place called Gethsemane, and he said to his disciples. 'Sit here, while I go over there and pray.' And taking with him Peter and the two sons of Zebedee, he began to be sorrowful and troubled. Then he said to them,

'My soul is very sorrowful, even to death; remain here, and watch with me.' And going a little farther he fell on his face and prayed, saying 'My Father, if it be possible, let this cup pass from me; nevertheless, not as I will, but as you will.' And he came to the disciples and found them sleeping. And he said to Peter, 'So, could you not watch with them one hour? Watch and pray that you may not enter into temptation. The spirit indeed is willing, but the flesh is weak.' Again, for the second time, he went away and prayed, 'My father, if this cannot pass until I drink it, your will be done.' And again he came and found them sleeping for their eyes were heavy. So, leaving them again, he went away and prayed for the third time, saying the same words again." Matthew 26:36-44 ESV.

Prostrate before the Father, voluntarily bearing the weight of human flesh, our beloved Savior writhed with emotions raw. As His human body wrestled with profound sorrow and turmoil, blood coursed as sweat down cheeks righteous. A plan woven from the beginning of time drew near completion, exacting a cost unimaginable yet yielding a blessing destined to reach the nations. Knowing in vivid clarity the path which stretched before, Jesus approached His Father, His flesh yearning for a change in the events to follow. A mission impossible to bear on human shoulders loomed upon a distant hill, bringing the crushing weight of humanity's transgressions and total separation from the Father. The perfect Lamb of God, Who knew no sin would become the true Passover Lamb, offering atonement undeserved to a creation trapped within their own desires. Within this passage, the enormity of the task and the ensuing sorrow lies palpable as the Savior seeks His Father. What a cost, a cost necessitated by our sin, distrust, and disobedience. Yet, what love shines forth upon that crown of thorns as the Father provides the ultimate payment to restore the relationships for which we were created. When faced with a creation in full rebellion, He chose to provide atonement through His Son rather than forced obedience to His will. In spite of the price, He will always provide a choice. How the Almighty must have grieved as events unfolded, knowing in His heart the cost accompanying the redemption He yearned to provide. Lying in submission before the Father, Jesus asked that the cup pass, not once but three times. While His flesh requested recourse, He remained submitted to the will of the Almighty, providing for all time the example of submission pure and true. "nevertheless, not as I will but as you will." (Matthew 26:39) Within these words lies the cornerstone of the gospel and the essence which often goes overlooked. Upon acceptance of the salvation offered, total, true submission is required, flowing forth to every recess of the heart. A heart change must occur, as our will succumbs to that of our new Father. A new being yearns for creation, one who lives only for His glory and walks with the beat of His heart, daily laying down his own life and desires in pursuit of the One who gave it all. Rather than mere belief, we must instead follow the spotless Lamb, treading daily in His footsteps and abiding in His example true and pure.

"Jesus said to her, 'Woman, believe me, the hour is coming when neither on this mountain nor in Jerusalem will you worship the Father. You worship what you do not know; we worship what we know, for salvation is from the Jews. The woman said to him, 'I know that Messiah is coming (he who is called Christ.) When he comes, he will tell us all things.' Jesus said to her, 'I who speak to you am he.'" John 4:21-22, 25-26.

His earthly body weary from travel, Jesus stopped aside a well near a town of Samaria, seeking rest and a divine appointment. Although the Samaritan woman searched for earthly water, what she found was without measure, for sitting beside the well was the Messiah foretold through the ages, the Source of living water to quench forevermore. As Jesus spoke, the true essence of the Father's plan was unveiled, a plan destined to bless the nations as pledged to Abraham. The redemption promised to reach the ends of the earth would flow through the Jews. "we worship what we know, for salvation is from the Jews." John 4:22 ESV. Do we truly know Who we worship? Do we embrace and understand the heritage of our Savior?

"Salvation is from the Jews." Wrapped within these five simple words rests intricacy inconceivable and a heart beating in fullness for His creation. As Jesus spoke with the Samaritan woman, the breath of life was again exhaled, revealing in clarity the source of all salvation. A plan meticulously woven from creation's breath poured forth in richness and beauty unimaginable, unveiling the mystery entwined through the ages and foretold by the prophets. Threads in the hands of the Master had traversed through ages past weaving continually a tapestry of redemption. Through all time and ages coursed His path of deliverance, revealed through the Law, cloaked as His Son in human flesh, outstretched upon a rudimentary cross, and wrapped lifeless within cloths of linen inside the tomb of Joseph of Arimathea. Within days of lying upon a floor of stone, the victory bought at a cost unimaginable burst forth, discarding strips of linen and revealing in fullness the tapestry of redemption completed through Jesus, the Jew. A loving Father waited forever near, beckoning and yearning for His creation, longing that they would know the depths of His love, heed His call, and recognize in fullness the plan woven with precision through the ages. As the reconciliation envisioned throughout time transitioned to reality, He pursued, drawing the created back to the Creator and the sinner back to the One who paid the ultimate cost. With outstretched arms and adorned with a crown of thorns, the very presence of God stretched forth through the body of a Jewish carpenter to bring salvation to a world replete with darkness.

When reviewed through the lens of Jewish heritage, the entirety of the Father's plan shines forth in richness and beauty indescribable. So, why was Jesus a Jew and what richness did His heritage yearn to impart? Although at times overlooked, salvation is wrapped within covenant, the template provided by the Almighty and used throughout ages past to reveal His design for relationship. Weaving days into centuries, a loving Father has stayed forever near, meticulously crafting a nation called by His name, a people created to be a nation of priests and destined to carry His covenant of promise to the world. Although His heart has longed always to bring redemption to the nations, His perfect design required the covenant to flow through the Jews. As foretold by the prophets of old, a Messiah would tread upon earthly soil, bringing the very presence of God to dwell amidst human souls. Outstretched upon a cross of wood, our beloved Savior, a Jew, provided the ultimate sacrifice through which we might be saved and through which we might enter into the covenant extended through the ages to the Jews. For any to receive the covenant of salvation, it must come through the precious blood of our Savior, Who descended cloaked in human flesh and lived within His full Jewish heritage.

As envisioned with creation's breath, a way was made for all, Jew and gentile alike, by which each might receive the redemption and restoration orchestrated throughout time. Through the death and resurrection of Jesus, gentiles have been graciously grafted into the nation chosen by the Father and granted a mission unique but equally valued. A beautiful day rests upon the horizon, a day when the loom of time will reveal in completeness the breadth of the Father's plan. For the tapestry to emerge in glorious entirety, all believers in Messiah must work together, walking in unity while remaining distinct in calling and purpose. Jew and gentile believers must abide fully in the One who provides their very breath, drawing sustenance from the roots of their faith and walking forward in the destinies for which they were created. With patience abounding, the Father waits. How He longs for all to feel the beat of His heart, to absorb the life of His breath, to answer the call He has woven through the centuries. As spoken through Paul in Romans 11, the gentiles have been granted a mission of utmost importance, a calling to spur the Jews to jealousy for their God. When they walk forward in their calling, the Jewish nation will return to the God of Israel and fulfill the destiny for which she was created, stepping forth as a nation of priests illuminating the love of the Father and ushering in a revival unlike any known before. A glorious day yearns to burst forth when all believers will walk together, distinct yet equally valued. As threads intertwine, the perfect will of our Father finds completion, revealing a tapestry of redemption offered to all and attained at a cost inconceivable. His heart yearns that all would know Him, that each would grasp in entirety the covenant extended, and that relationships would be restored. How He has pursued, planned, and waited with a love that knows no end.

We owe our salvation to Jesus, the Jew. Pause and inhale the breath of the Father. Feel the life He longs to deliver. Allow His pulse to course through your veins, nourishing with the full heritage of our Messiah and delivering the living water to sustain forevermore. Remember always the source from

Whom our salvation flows. Without a covenant, salvation is not found. Without a Jew, there is no covenant. Without belief in the death and resurrection of Jesus, the King of the Jews, salvation remains undelivered. When we embrace the heritage of our Savior, the heart of our Father shines forth in vibrancy and depth previously unknown. As He walked upon earthly shores, He was known by the Hebrew name *Yeshua*, which is short for *Yehoshua* and means *the Lord is salvation*.[10] Pause and inhale the Jewish identity of our Savior, embrace the covenant which has been graciously offered, and grasp in entirety the fullness of the Master's plan. Allow the heritage of our Messiah and the roots supporting the Christian faith to deliver the nourishment He longs to impart. Desiring relationship, obedience, and love above all, the Father has gone to enormous lengths to reveal His plan of redemption, to restore to us the opportunity to walk with Him in fellowship, and to save us from ourselves. Let us choose rightly and never take lightly the covenant offered at a staggering cost. Throughout time, He has remained forever near, weaving a beautiful tapestry of redemption within the thread of Jewish history and heritage. Let us as Christians return to the roots of our faith and remember always the One who supports our very existence and through Whom our salvation flows.

"Long ago in many times and in many ways, God spoke to our fathers by the prophets, but in these last days he has spoken us by his Son, whom he appointed the heir of all things, through whom also he created the world. He is the radiance

[10] Ron Cantor, Identity Theft, 78.

of the glory of God and the exact imprint of his nature, and he upholds the universe by the word of his power. After making purification for sins, he sat down at the right hand of the Majesty on high, having become as much superior to the angels as the name he has inherited is more excellent than theirs." Hebrews 1:1-4 ESV.

Son of God

Jesus of Nazareth

the King of the Jews

Yeshua HaMashiach

(Jesus the Messiah)

20

The Lord's Feasts and Festivals

Tapestry Of Roots: Threads Woven By The Master

English Name	Feast
Passover	Pesach
Unleavened Bread	Chag haMatzot
First Fruits	Reshiyt K'tzir'chem or Yom HaBikuriym
Pentecost or the Feast of Weeks	Shavuot

Meaning	Gregorian & Hebrew Dates
Passover remembers God passing over the houses of the Israelites in Egypt and the Israelites' deliverance from Egypt. It also marks the beginning of the Biblical year. Jesus as the Passover Lamb is the fulfillment of Passover.	March / April 14th of Nisan
The Feast of Unleavened Bread recalls the Israelites' hasty deliverance from Egypt and calls to mind the issue of sin within our lives.	March / April 14th - 21st of Nisan
The Feast of First Fruits celebrates the first harvest of the season, which was traditionally the barley harvest. Today, it recalls Jesus' resurrection as "the firsttfruits of those who have fallen asleep" 1 Corinthians 15:20.	March / April 16th of Nisan
Traditionally, the Feast of Shavuot celebrated the first wheat harvest of the year. Shavuot is also connected to the giving of the Law on Mount Sinai and to the outpouring of the Holy Spirit in Acts 2.	May / June 6th of Sivan

English Name	Feast
Feast of Trumpets	Rosh Hashanah or Yom Teru'ah
Day of Atonement	Yom Kippur
Feast of Booths / Feast of Tamernacles	Sukkot

Meaning	Gregorian & Hebrew Dates
The Feast of Trumpets is the first of the fall feasts and is celebrated with the blowing of the shofar. It later expanded into a celebration of the new year. Today, this feast provides hope in the return of our Savior.	September / October 1st of Tishri
Celebrated as the holiest day of the year, Yom Kippur was the one time each year when the high priest would enter the Holy of Holies to make atonement for the people of Israel. Today, we see the death and resurrection of Jesus as our salvation and the fulfillment of the sacrificial requirements.	September / October 10th of Tishri
Sukkot, the final wheat harvest of the season, recalls the Israelites' 40 years of wandering in the wilderness and the provision of the Father throughout. Today, it calls to mind the temporary nature of our life on earth and the presence of the Holy Spirit dwelling within believers.	September / October 15-21st of Tishri

For additional information concerning the Biblical Feasts and Festivals, see:

The Messianic Jewish Family Bible, Tree of Life Version, published by the Messianic Jewish Family Bible Society, 2015.

21

Concluding Thoughts

So, a book about covenants?

Can you see it now?

Relevance does, indeed, remain.

While our world swirls in instant reality, the key to our very existence lies within relationships. Stretched upon a rudimentary cross, a Jewish Savior paid the ultimate cost to allow the restoration of relationships envisioned with creation's breath. The heart of our Father yearns for His creation, desiring relationships between His people as well as with Himself. As time has coursed through ages past and present, He has stood forever near, orchestrating heaven and earth while weaving a tapestry of redemption. He has pursued, revealed His heart, poured forth His love, and proven Himself trustworthy, faithful, and pure. Longing to reside within our very beings, He stretched forth cloaked in humanity, yearning to touch each deeply and exhale the breath of life into our innermost recesses. Within the stillness, He waits with arms outstretched and a heart beating for all. Desiring relationships above all, He asks …..

If I invite you, …..

will you come?

The Almighty yearns for relationship with you.

In the midst of distractions innumerable, the quiet whisper begs an audience, inviting you to relationship and covenant with the very Creator of the universe. He stands ready, longing for you to grasp the covenant extended so that you might walk forth in the victory attained at the cross and thrive in the destiny for which you were created.

If I invite you, ...

will you embrace My full identity?

He waits patiently for the day when we cherish His complete identity, absorb the essence of His heritage, and receive the gifts He longs to bestow. Wrapped within His identity lies completeness unimaginable, love unfathomed, and devotion pure. Open your heart to embrace the entirety of your Savior, for within covenant will you find relationship like no other, relationship true and pure. Much lies wrapped within the context of His heritage, as no detail passes without meaning and significance. A plan orchestrated meticulously throughout all time weaves a tapestry of redemption offered to all through covenant.

Because of His perfect design, the pull of relationships remains unyielding and yearns for restoration. One day, the body of believers will tread united, Jew and gentile together, seeing in clarity the missions to which they have been called and walking forth in their full identities. As awareness dawns, the gentile believers will shine forth His heart in truth and fullness, spurring the Jews to jealousy for their God and provoking a return unprecedented. Israel, a nation crafted by the very hand of the Almighty with a mission and purpose irrevocable, will burst forth as a nation of priests, ushering in a revival unlike any other. Israel has been a nation persecuted but protected, blamed and misunderstood but preserved, stiff-necked and struggling but still standing; Israel will yet be redeemed.

If I invite you, …..

will you return?

How he longs for us to return to the roots of our faith, to truly know Him in His fullness and grasp the desires of His heart within our beings. Once we return to the roots of our faith, we discover a Father whose love for us knows no bounds, Who desires us above all else. As days weave into centuries, He remains forever near offering the chance to return and desiring that all would know the one true heart that beats always for them. The invitation awaits. Receive the covenant offered at the highest of costs and thrive within true relationship created, ordained, and perfected since the beginning of time. Remember always the roots of your faith and embrace the heritage of the One from Whom all things flow.

The Father beckons …

Return …

to Me, to covenant, to your roots.

22

Recommended Reading

Recommended Reading

Cantor, Ron. *Identity Theft*. Shippensburg, PA: Destiny Image Pub., 2013. Print.

Finto, Don. *Your People Shall Be My People*. Ventura, CA: Regal, 2001. Print.

Hettinga, Jan David. *Follow Me, Experience the Loving Leadership of Jesus*. United States: NavPress, 1996. Print.

Intrater, Asher. *Who Ate Lunch With Abraham?: A Study of the Appearances of God in the Form of a Man in the Hebrew Scriptures*. United States: Intermedia Public Relations, 2011. Print.

Intrater, Keith. *Covenant Relationships: A More Excellent Way: A Handbook for Integrity and Loyalty in the Body of Christ*. Shippensburg, PA: Destiny Image, 1989. Print.

Juster, Daniel C. *Growing to Maturity: A Messianic Jewish Guide*. Gaithersburg, MD: Union of Messianic Congregations, 1987. Print.

Juster, Daniel C. *The Irrevocable Calling: Israel's Role as a Light to the Nations*. Clarksville, MD: Messianic Jewish, 2007. Print.

Juster, Daniel C. *Jewish Roots: A Foundation of Biblical Theology*. Shippensburg, PA: Destiny Image, 1995. Print.

Schiffman, Michael. *Return of the Remnant: The Rebirth of Messianic Judaism*. Baltimore, MD: Lederer Messianic, 1996. Print.

What About the New Covenant? First Fruits of Zion, Inc. Audio Lecture Series. Presented by D. Thomas Lancaster. 2014.

Order Information

Book orders may be placed through our website at:

www.tapestryofrootsorders.com

Bulk Orders

If you would like to purchase a bulk order for your discussion group or Bible class, orders of 10 or more books may be purchased at 20% off. Please go to our website and click the order link in the navigation bar to place your bulk order.

www.tapestryofrootsorders.com

Messianic Publishers, LLC
Memphis, TN U.S.A.

Tapestry Of Roots: Threads Woven By The Master

9 780988 892095